101

WAYS TO REINVEST YOUR LIFE

STEVE AND JANIE SJOGREN

NAVPRESS

Bringing Truth to Life
P.O. Box 35001, Colorado Springs, Colorado 80935

OUR GUARANTEE TO YOU

We believe so strongly in the message of our books that we are making this quality guarantee to you. If for any reason you are disappointed with the content of this book, return the title page to us with your name and address and we will refund to you the list price of the book. To help us serve you better, please briefly describe why you were disappointed. Mail your refund request to: NavPress, P.O. Box 35002, Colorado Springs, CO 80935.

The Navigators is an international Christian organization. Our mission is to reach, disciple, and equip people to know Christ and to make Him known through successive generations. We envision multitudes of diverse people in the United States and every other nation who have a passionate love for Christ, live a lifestyle of sharing Christ's love, and multiply spiritual laborers among those without Christ.

NavPress is the publishing ministry of The Navigators. NavPress publications help believers learn biblical truth and apply what they learn to their lives and ministries. Our mission is to stimulate spiritual formation among our readers.

© 2003 by Steve and Janie Sjogren
www.navpress.com
ISBN 1-57683-229-5

Cover design by Jennifer Mahalik
Cover photos by Adobe Image Library
Creative Team: Brad Lewis, Amy Spencer, Pat Miller

Some of the anecdotal illustrations in this book are true to life and are included with the permission of the persons involved. All other illustrations are composites of real situations, and any resemblance to people living or dead is coincidental.

Unless otherwise identified, all Scripture quotations in this publication are taken from the HOLY BIBLE: NEW INTERNATIONAL VERSION® (NIV®). Copyright © 1973, 1978, 1984 by International Bible Society. Used by permission of Zondervan Publishing House. All rights reserved. Other versions used is the *New King James Version* (NKJV). Copyright © 1982 by Thomas Nelson, Inc. Used by permission. All rights reserved.

Sjogren, Steve, 1955-
  101 ways to reinvest your life / Steve and Janie Sjogren.
    p. cm.
  ISBN 1-57683-229-5
  1. Retirees--Religious life. 2. Retirement--Religious
aspects--Christianity. 3. Vocation--Christianity. 4. Retirees in
church work. I. Title: One hundred and one ways to reinvest your life.
II. Title: One hundred one ways to reinvest your life. III. Sjogren,
Janie, 1954- IV. Title.
  BV4596.R47 S56 2003
  331.7'02'0846--dc21

                                    2003015983

Printed in the United States of America

1 2 3 4 5 6 7 8 9 10 / 07 06 05 04 03

FOR ROSE "TIPSY" PURMORT

You are the consummate "reinvestor."
Thank you for being a model to all at Vineyard
Community Church. May we all become like you—
faithful stewards throughout life!

CONTENTS

FINANCIAL

INTRODUCTION

So, WHY ARE YOU reading this book? Maybe you're at a point of exploration—seeking out the dreams of your heart. You're asking the question, "How can I best spend my life from this point forward?"

We call that "reinvesting." Whether you're retiring, beginning your empty-nest years, or at some other crossroads, as a "reinvestor" you're more interested in making a difference than in making a living. You're even willing to work for less pay—or in some cases, no pay—but for far more meaning.

Just what makes you tick? You want to find a meaningful place to give your life away to others. You want to change the world—even if it's just one other person's world. No matter what your age or position in life, if you get to the place where you regularly give of yourself in significant ways to others, you'll experience God's richest blessings.

Take retirement. This concept is changing rapidly. Part of that change is being driven by the astronomical retirement rate of the baby boom generation. Baby boomers consistently redefine every social structure they pass through in life. Just as members of this generation redefine the institutions of dating, education, marriage, and family life, they'll certainly redefine retirement. Currently, nearly eleven thousand Americans reach their fiftieth birthday each day,[1] so the force behind the change is significant.

The classic view of retirement—stopping work, taking it easy, pursuing the easy life of golf, sailing, and moving to a condo in Florida—is changing. After their pensions kick in and they have access to their IRAs, people want their lives to be fruitful. They want to make a difference in the world. Many boomers are even retiring early.

A generation ago, the gnawing question in retirement was, "How can I have fun in the last part of my life?" Now the question is, "How can I make the last part of my life the most redemptive part of my life? How can I most profoundly serve others now that I've accumulated a lifetime of experiences and skills?" Or as a friend of mine aptly puts it, "How can I make the rest of my life the best of my life?"

It's no longer about *re*tirement. It's all about *pro*-tirement.

Reinvesting is about recovering—regaining all the spent

energy you've put out during your decades of living, working, and growing wiser through life's ups and downs.

Pro-tirement means going full force into the future toward whatever energizes you. It's laying aside all encumbrances that kept you from engaging in becoming the real you. Pro-tirement means joyfully expending great levels of energy to express Christ's love to the world.

Lilly found herself at a crossroad in life at the age of fifty-one. She was making good money as a legal secretary. Her children were raised and through college. Her marriage had recently failed. Life was presenting itself to her in the form of a question: "What do you want to do with the rest of your life—make money, or pursue the desires of your heart?"

Lilly felt like a fully fueled rocket on the launching pad that never got off the ground. When she asked, "What fuels me?" the answer was easy enough. For years she had been pursuing her passion at arts festivals. She was a gifted storyteller. So she enrolled in a communications program and now, four years later, she's become a full-fledged professional storyteller. She says, "It's no longer a money thing—it's all about passion in life. I wouldn't trade it for anything!"

For the purposes of this book, let's restate our definition. "Reinvestors" refers to people about forty and older who've decided to pursue an alternative to traditional retirement. Whether retired yet or not, they're beginning to have more free time and they want to use it wisely. Instead of going off into the sunset in their golden years, these people are finding useful ministry to do that betters the world and the people around them.

DARE TO D-R-E-A-M!

Our dreams shape us. When unleashed upon the world, a dream is a powerful thing. If we don't express our dreams, we become frustrated. A wise man said, "Hope deferred makes the heart sick" (Proverbs 13:12).

Reinvesting your life to make a difference is about dreaming. Perhaps you've had a dream growing inside you for years. But things got in the way—life got in the way. Things are different now. You have time to catch your breath and think with a new attitude and a new perspective.

If you dream boldly, you'll set great forces in motion in your life. Consider the following D-R-E-A-M acrostic as the basis for the dream you need to dream.

Determine to be true to yourself. You'll always feel pressure in the modern rush of life to compromise your true calling—to give in to the pressure of things that are put upon you in the name of efficiency. But you have a unique dream; you're the only one in the world with this dream. God wants to express his one-of-a-kind dream for you, through you. You're the only person on the planet who can live out this dream. God gave you a specialized calling and opportunity at this point in your life. Take it seriously and go for it with the open doors God provides.

People entering ministry in the second half of life often comment that they feel "so alive." That's true. In so many cases we are, for the first time, entering into our vocation in the truest sense of the word. Vocation is our true ministry life as opposed to our occupation—what we do (or did) in order to keep bread on the table. Now it's time to put aside our preoccupation with our occupation and pay attention to our heart's true desire for a life vocation.

Resolve to pursue the dream God put in your heart. This involves coming to the place where you declare, "Now is the time. This is the place. I am the person." Perhaps you've thought about your dream for years. At other times it was impossible for you to say yes to your dream. "Later" may not work either. Go for it now while the time is right, while the door is open before you.

God formed you so that he might fulfill you as you pursue this dream. Part of the missing element in your life has been the "walking out" of this plan. In a sense, this is the culmination of your life's direction. And it's a glorious beginning.

Not sure what dreams lie dormant in your heart? Ask God and keep your eyes open. What moves you? What are you glad you made time to do in your life so far? What do you consider "time well spent"? What have you done that may have eternal results? Answers to these questions will give you clues to your gifts, passions, and dreams.

Engage. Just start in the journey. Begin your future now. Decide that it all starts right here, right now. If not now, when? If not you, who? Don't put off any longer what has been brewing in you for years. God put together a unique package for you. You now have the desire, the time, the life experiences, and the economic and physical means to pull off this incredible dream. What's left to do but to go for it?

Many of us learned faulty lessons in life—that we ought to hesitate, take it slow, and not make any moves until we're absolutely certain that we're going to see success. That's the thinking of people who've talked themselves into believing that they have unlimited opportunity. Now you're old enough to know that isn't true. Opportunity has a way of passing by. Instead of following the marching orders of "Ready, aim, ready, aim," change your cadence to "ready, fire!, aim."

Arrange your life around your dream. Reinvestors are irrepressibly enthusiastic people because they focus their energies solely on their reason for living—their gift to others that flows through them. Set up things so that your life absolutely serves and supports your dream. Your resources must rally around that dream. It must become the priority of your life. Living your life around your dream means making it much more than a hobby; it becomes a comprehensive, all-engaging lifestyle.

In the interviews we conducted with reinvestors during the research of this book, we heard the same phrase over and over: "I have a unique opportunity!" Reinvestors see their lives as a blessing from God, a gift from the Holy Spirit in the form of open doors and unlimited opportunities.

Think of all the times in the past when you have done things that you weren't "about." It's time for a change. You can now focus on the one thing you can build your life upon—the thing God has given you to do.

Maryann worked at a bank for years, doing various jobs throughout the organization. She was well liked and naturally worked her way up in the business by doing a little bit of everything. Her family's financial situation got to the point where she no longer needed to work, so she began to make plans for retiring at age forty and pursuing her full-time passion: praying for people. She's been doing just that for about ten years, "working" at least a forty-hour-per-week prayer schedule. She conducts prayer training, she spends regularly scheduled prayer hours at her church, she coordinates a prayer chain, and she's part of a vital network of teams that pray for people in need. She stays so busy she is now "good tired" most of the time and deeply satisfied with her new career.

Reinvestors have learned to network their relationships and resources to get the most out of what they have. They might not have unlimited resources, but they seem to have unlimited creativity for connecting and investing what they do have.

Manage by becoming a steward of the dream God has given you. Remember, you didn't just think up this dream for yourself. Instead, God's fingerprints are all over it! He put this idea in your mind and inspired it into life in your heart. It's a holy and sacred thing; treat it with proper care and respect.

God also gives you resources to spend on your dream—resources that normally wouldn't be available. But now they're present in your life because God has something special for you to redeem them on—something that's going to change the world. Spend your resources well, for God has a great purpose for your life and the task at hand: to bless and touch the lives of others in profound ways. Always keep before you the larger purpose of God: to change the world through your gifts.

Part of the task God is calling you to is to direct the people you serve back to him. Each idea in this book serves as an icebreaker for you to enter into the lives of those you touch. As you share your gift, you'll have the opportunity to share why you're doing it. You simply need to direct people back to Christ: "I do this to show God's love in a practical way!"

God's love always arrives in tangible ways. He has given you something real to share with the world. Your life opens doors to God's kingdom for others to walk through. Use it boldly!

"AND ONE" PEOPLE

A new line of clothing and shoes has recently become popular. It's called "And One." The name is connected to the idea that the basketball players who use these products will be so skilled they'll be able to score the regular shot—and then draw a foul shot beyond that. Thus, the "And One" name. It's another way of saying, "We're fulfilling the regular expectations of life and then gaining points beyond that! We're good at what we do because we've lived long and learned much about the game of life."

This book is about finding success after you've already found success. It may mean that you finally find success after not feeling all that fulfilled in the work world. The sense of attainment that eluded you will manifest itself in the second half of life through your *real* work in life. Being an "And One" person means finding what you are for and then going for that with all the gusto that comes your way as you pursue reinvesting your life.

One of the wisest things anyone ever said to me (Steve) came from a mentor who thought I was taking myself too seriously at too young an age. I was twenty-four at the time and thought I was getting old and should be doing what I was supposed to be doing in life. As John Wayne put it in *The Cowboys,* I thought I was "burning daylight." But my friend saw it much differently. He was growing weary of my too-serious mood. One day he'd had too much and said, "Look, Sjogren, you're way too serious. Here's the way it is: People aren't worth listening to until they're at least thirty. They're not worth reading until they're at least forty. And they don't know what their purpose in life is until they're at least fifty. If you know what you're about by the time you reach your mid-fifties, you'll be way ahead of the pack."

The older I've gotten, the more those words make sense to me.

Don't feel bad if you haven't discovered your purpose by the time you reach fifty. Even if you haven't reached your stride by then, it's okay. This book may help you take the first steps on the journey to finding your life's true meaning—to discovering your authentic vocation after retiring from or cutting back on your regular occupation.

TIPS FOR EFFECTIVE REINVESTING EXPERIENCES

These ideas are the accumulation of conversations with several dozen reinvestors who've had fulfilling volunteer experiences with churches and other organizations. Where better to learn how to live an effective second half of life than from people who've successfully transitioned into that phase?

Get a Realistic Assessment of Your Lifelong Learnings

Take a look at yourself. What do you like to do? Do you like to work with people, paper, or things? Are you an extrovert or an introvert? Are you more excited about putting things in order or creating new things? Some people are great at thinking up new things, creating explosions of ideas, but they're not good at the details of organizing the results. Others are great at creating systems to clean up the messiness that comes with a new idea or endeavor.

Others are best at maintaining systems that are already in place.

Are you best at the explosion, the setting in order, or the maintenance? Steve is a man of ideas, explosions, and starting things. Janie is more of an efficiency expert, making order and creating systems for things to run more smoothly. Neither of us likes to maintain systems once they're in place.

Find someone to assess you—to help figure you out. What strengths and weaknesses do you bring into reinvesting? A job or outplacement counselor can do a good job at this sort of evaluation.

Take the Myers-Briggs Type Indicator test. A shortened version of this can be found in the book *Please Understand Me II* by David Keirsey (Prometheus Nemesis Books, 1988). This material will help you get a clearer grasp on where you fit into the organization you're thinking of working with, and it will help make that relationship as seamless as possible.

Be Open to More Learning and Training

Reinvestors are lifelong learners. Consider going back to school, whether formally or informally. Informal training might include leadership development or classes in facilitating groups or in listening. Formal training might be in computer or technical skills, or in new fields you have interest in.

You're not too old to go back to college if the opportunity presents itself. One person we interviewed started learning Spanish at age seventy and took up the flute at seventy-five! He became proficient at both by the time he reached a mere eighty years of age! A short stint in a Toastmasters International club might be just what you need if you see public speaking in your future. These groups do excellent training in beginning a talk, engaging a group, getting to the point, making your talk interesting, and closing it before you lose the group's attention. (See their website, www.toastmasters.org, for some great speaking tips that will help anyone learn more about making presentations.)

It's vital to know our strengths and weaknesses, yet we must never think that we can't learn anything new. Part of the vision for a reinvesting ministry is realizing that we'll be stretched beyond where we've been and into new places in life. We need to become comfortable being somewhat uncomfortable.

You won't always match your previous background directly with your new ministry as a reinvestor. Retired teachers will not necessarily teach as reinvestors. They may have had their fill of teaching and desire to get into a completely different area of interest. They might study an area of technical interest and become proficient enough to be able to help others in that area. Someone who possesses significant technical prowess may want nothing to do with the technical side of things later in life. Steve's mother, Glenna, spent most of her working life in the medical field, but at age seventy she wanted a change. Now retired, she regularly travels with us on ministry trips, actively grandparents with a passion, and has begun to take art classes (she's very good). She chooses to reinvest her life in people and things she loves.

One thing's for sure — we're perpetual students. We read. We study people and life with a passion because we understand that effectiveness in life and effectiveness in ministry are one and the same thing.

Seek Out Other Reinvestors for Encouragement and Fellowship

While reinvesting jobs can be exciting and fulfilling, it can be a lonely path as well. You need fellowship and prayer support from others who are doing similar things, who can empathize with your situation. Strength and encouragement come in numbers.

You'll naturally gravitate toward others who are in the same boat as you. If some sort of support group for reinvestors doesn't exist, start one for people at your church or in your social group who are ruminating around the message of this book.

Work for Free If You Can Afford It

When you work in a reinvesting position, don't be surprised if you're offered a paid position with the organization or people you're serving. We encourage you to say politely, "No thanks." Being hired changes the dynamic completely; moving from volunteer to employee violates the spirit of what it is to be a person in the reinvesting stage. There's something wonderful about being freely connected to an organization and not entangled in financial webs.

At Vineyard Community Church in Cincinnati we have what we call "senior staff." This is for people over forty who've already played out a career in the work world and who want something more fulfilling in ministry. Most of these people work for free, while some are paid a part-time wage to supplement their fixed incomes. If you do need an income, you might approach the organizations where you hope to work with the idea of being paid a small stipend to maintain the feel of being a reinvestor.

Realize This Involves a Change of View: You're Now Primarily a Giver

Life is so often all about *me*. But when you hit the reinvestor stage, that doesn't hold true any longer. Now it's all about *them*.

How do you respond when you hear that truth? Maybe you're in pain and don't feel you can afford to give of yourself yet. That's fine. Be honest. Address the areas of your life that need healing—and get help. That help might be in the form of a book, a seminar, a twelve-step program, a retreat, a great sermon, or professional therapy. Wherever you are, take steps to bring more healing and personal growth into your life.

Kathy is a single mom who found herself divorced, an empty nester, and empty emotionally. Her health was failing to the point that she was unable to pursue her career as a nurse. Depression subtly settled into her life. She began to feel as though no one needed her—not even her children. Her emotional state came to a head one day when she found it impossible to get out of bed. In the depths of her despair, she wondered if it was worth it to ever get out of bed. Realizing she needed help, she went to church and asked for prayer. Janie ended up praying for her.

Kathy assumed that Janie might be able to relate to her suffering in light of Steve's long-term physical ailments, which were brought on by a botched surgery several years ago. Janie affirmed Kathy's thoughts: Sometimes life stinks and usually no easy answers exist. Yet, while you can't control the things life throws at you, you can at least control your response to your circumstances.

This prayer encounter began a renovation within Kathy. She began to stop looking at everything wrong in her life. She got the focus off herself. She enrolled in a growth group. She began to volunteer almost daily, using her secretarial skills at the church. Now she not only answers phones, she also offers hope to others by taking part in the ministry team that helps people in the church's Divorce and Beyond ministry.

Avoid People Who Are Retreating from Life and Calling It "Retirement"

People who pursue the traditional way of retirement will get you down. They don't understand the idea of giving yourself to others in meaningful ways. What you want to do mystifies those who haven't yet grasped the concept of reinvesting instead of retiring.

You're following a radically different paradigm when you pursue the pro-tirement perspective. It's as different as night is from day—as spending is from investing. Live out your pro-tirement with great enthusiasm. If you meet curiosity seekers along the way, and if they "get" what you're doing, fine. Otherwise, go your way. Life's too short to have to explain and defend yourself constantly.

Understand That You're Operating out of a Covenant, Not a Career

Many people don't understand the difference between a career and a vocation based on a covenant relationship between God and us. Again, the differences are as stark as night and day.

Career— Making a Living	Covenant— Making a Difference
It has a beginning and an ending point.	It has a beginning but no end.
It's an independent decision made by someone.	It's an agreement between two parties—God and you.
It's something you have to work at to feel energy for.	It's the reason you live. It brings life to your existence.
It's human in origin.	It's between God and you. You signed up for a lifelong term.
It's self-originated.	It's divinely originated; the greater party (God) seeks out the lesser (you).

God had in mind that work would be something sacred. It was meant to be a gift from him—not just something we do to keep body and soul together. God ordained that a large percentage of our lives would be spent at work, so he sought to make it meaningful and fulfilling to us.

But if we don't seek the strength of a covenant life, we can't live the sort of relaxed life God wants us to live. Without a covenant, all we have left is striving and perpetual struggle—something we weren't designed to bear emotionally.

Though she had a good-paying job, Karen felt called to abandon the asphalt jungle to work in a suburban high school as a "bouncer." Her job is to monitor halls and make sure students make it to class. Though she's had her moments over the years, she thinks the cut in pay has been more than worth it in the long run.

She approaches her job from a spiritual perspective. She prays daily for all the kids. She prays constantly as she roams the halls looking for out-of-place students.

One girl who was a regular on the truant list seven years ago was also a regular on Karen's prayer list. Recently, this girl has begun to attend Karen's church and is now a volunteer youth leader. Karen is seeing the fruits of her decision right in front of her eyes!

Don't Allow Yourself to Be Dismayed

You'll probably be discouraged when you first offer your service. Most organizations/church systems/congregations/people don't know how to respond to *any* volunteers, much less the specialized people who are reinvestors. Take heart. You'll be paving the way for others who'll follow in your footsteps. As the idea catches on through you, others will want to get in on a good thing. And the organization will also see the great value you're offering—one too good not to pass on.

Realize You Might Be More Skilled Than the People You're Working With

You'll certainly have more life experiences than the people you work with. So how do you do this work with the right attitude? Smile—a lot! And remember why you're doing this—to glorify God. It's not a job. You already went through that in the previous part of your life. Nor are you seeking to get some sort of identity; you're through with that part of your life too (hopefully!). You're here to serve. You're here to advance the kingdom of God!

WHAT IT TAKES TO BE A REINVESTOR

Imagination

It takes skill to be able to take the reality that is and make it into something greater. In other words, it takes great ability to see beyond what is and into what could be. We need to be able to see the bigger picture of what God has in mind. God seems to give greater vision as people move into the reinvesting zone.

Willingness to Work Hard
If you bought this book, you're probably not afraid of hard work. The title includes the implication of getting to work.

You've probably worked hard for someone else for decades, doing something that wasn't all that fulfilling. How much more are you willing to work hard at the ministry God has created you to do?

Of all the reinvestors we met while writing this book, not a single one was afraid of hard work. They all seemed to become more fulfilled as they gave themselves wholeheartedly to the work God called them to.

An Enduring Spirit
After you read this book, you may start a new ministry from scratch. There's always the price of a pound of flesh to pay for that sort of start-up ministry. People won't understand what you're trying to do. You'll invariably do a lot of explaining and a fair amount of hand holding as you work to get your new ministry off the ground. While it's obvious to you why the ministry is necessary, others might not see it so clearly. It will even blow your mind that while you're volunteering to better the church in a strong way, church leaders may make you answer questions that seem to call into account whether this ministry is even valid. But that's just what you'll have to do—at first anyway.

We know this sounds frustrating. After a while, you just get used to being in a place of misunderstanding. Welcome to the club of the pioneer—the place where people start things!

Intrinsic Motivation
You won't have much public recognition as a reinvestor. You'll encounter misunderstanding. You probably won't be thanked much or often by the people you're serving. This ministry requires that you "serve wholeheartedly, as if you were serving the Lord, not men, because you know that the Lord will reward everyone for whatever good he does" (Ephesians 6:7-8).

God will open doors of opportunity before you. Your work is definitely not about money! It's about fulfillment. And mostly it's about serving the purposes of God through an attitude of availability.

We list these projects to get your juices flowing. They're springboards for thousands of more ideas to help you step outside the circle of your everyday life and begin to intentionally connect with others for the purpose of making a difference in their lives. Loneliness, isolation, and boredom are easy lifestyles to slip into. It takes a proactive step outward to break that cycle.

Reinvesting is a new way to look at life. Reinvest your time, energy, and life experiences for eternal rewards. Let's get started!

BUSINESS

1 BUSINESS "LAUNCHER"

Some veteran business people have the ability to take novice small-business people under their wings and help them get off the ground when they're starting a new business. Some have a gift to be parental figures, helping those who are less experienced in business. Men and women who've successfully started businesses not only have the technical knowledge to get a thriving concern going, but they also have something beyond value: the ability to give away confidence. For a young entrepreneur, confidence is a commodity with a value beyond words. Successful business leaders impart confidence in simple ways—by spending time with the people they're mentoring, by answering questions that come up in the natural course of a conversation, and by sharing stories from their own experiences. There's nothing like the firsthand story of struggle, failure, and ultimate success to build up someone's courage.

GIFTS/SKILLS/EXPERIENCES

- Teaching
- Leadership
- Mentoring
- Business
- Venture capitalist

Here are a few ways you can help:

- Give insights about raising money to someone in a dead-end financial situation.
- Help someone learn how to operate a business in a developing country.
- Share the secrets of how to find financing for a business start-up.
- Help a budding entrepreneur turn a dream into a solid business plan.

One of the main reasons businesses fail is a lack of planning. You can help the business leaders of the near future think through the basics of starting a business with increased chances to succeed.

How to Get Started

Join a local service organization such as Rotary or Kiwanis. There are plenty of people hanging out at these meetings who need mentoring or encouragement.

2 SMALL-BUSINESS COACH

When it comes to the business world, why think in terms of the secular-vs.-sacred divide? If you're a Christian business leader, you have a lot to contribute to leaders of small businesses. As a successful business owner, you have confidence and an established track record. That gives you credibility.

GIFTS/SKILLS/EXPERIENCES

- Patience
- Vision
- Verbal skills
- Business
- Mentoring
- Career counseling

For a variety of reasons, most small businesses don't make it past the first couple of years of existence. Struggling owners who have a coach providing direction and encouragement can jump ahead of their competition.

Serve as a cheerleader by creating a support group for people starting a new business. Meet centrally at breakfast or lunchtime to discuss relevant topics.

- Discuss businesses that are at a turning point.
- Take turns leading the group.
- Bring in outside speakers to share inspiring stories.
- Keep the speaking to no more than fifteen minutes, and include a question-and-answer period with time for discussion.
- Encourage networking.
- Mail or e-mail encouraging training materials to group members between meetings.

How to Get Started

Advertise in your church's newsletter or bulletin and/or put a blurb in local newspapers. Be sure to include what, where, when, and how interested participants can contact you.

3 OUTREACH DIRECTOR TO THE BUSINESS COMMUNITY

Churches commonly have outreach directors focused on their communities. Why not create an outreach director to the business community? If you already have a foothold in the business world, you can find dozens of creative ways to build bridges into that world.

For a number of years, I (Steve) ran a fax newsletter called *Focused Life Fax*. I sent it to several hundred businesses throughout the Cincinnati area. It was popular and well received by the business community.

Here are a few other ways you can reach out to the business community:

Gifts/Skills/Experiences

- Evangelism
- Encouragement
- Leadership
- Pastoral care
- Mentoring
- Business

- Hold breakfast or lunch meetings to offer spiritual encouragement and opportunities for networking.
- Form breakfast and lunch Bible study and discipleship groups.
- Offer to pray for issues members of the business community are facing.
- Hold meetings for several small-business starters to create fellowship opportunities.

How to Get Started
Advertise in your church's bulletin and in local or regional business publications.

4 PALM PILOT CONSULTANT

Millions of people have Palm Pilots and similar devices—probably you included! You know how handy they are. And you may also know how incredibly frustrating they can be when they malfunction. Nothing is more exasperating than seeing several weeks of scheduling and planning go down the drain when the "error" screen appears on your Personal Digital Assistant (PDA).

I (Steve) have had fourteen of these devices over the past seven years. Okay, I've dropped a few and I've outgrown several. I've had difficulties on a regular basis. But few paid consultants exist to fix PDA problems—no one's in the phone book to call when you need help.

You can become fluent in Palm Operating System and in the latest software and upgrades by reading books and practicing on your own PDA. Become an expert by experiment and experience. Then put the word out that you're open for business, and you'll soon have plenty of customers coming to you.

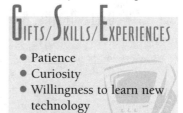

Gifts/Skills/Experiences
- Patience
- Curiosity
- Willingness to learn new technology
- Technical ability
- Knowledge of Palm OS

This ministry could generate a lot of interest because no formal means exists for getting this work done. You could have more business than you can deal with realistically. You can team up with others to spread out the work and share the blessings of ministry.

How to Get Started

Advertise in computer stores and giveaway newspapers. Connect with pastors and missionaries who are Palm users.

5 COMPUTER REPAIR TECHNICIAN

Most homes have at least one computer; ours has five! The more computers you own, the more goes wrong. After fiddling with computers for years, we've become convinced that the adage is true: they're built to become obsolete after eighteen months.

If you've ever had your own computer woes, you know it's expensive to have a professional come to your home to do hardware and software repair and tweaking. Many people depend on friends who seem to know what they're doing.

GIFTS/SKILLS/EXPERIENCES

- Serving
- Technical ability
- Communication skills
- Computer services

If you've developed a knack for fixing computer problems through the years, develop a ministry built around it! You'll need to set boundaries because people will call you back over and over again. Set a "once-a-month" policy—you'll work on their computers just once each month.

How to Get Started
Place flyers at computer stores and at your church, and put announcements in giveaway newspapers.

6 WEBSITE DESIGNER

We're not website designers. But we know a number of people who are. They assure us that designing and maintaining sites are acquired skills that have less to do with the technical end of computers and more to do with the ability to see patterns and the flow of information.

GIFTS/SKILLS/EXPERIENCES

- Serving
- Patience
- Creativity
- Vision
- Graphic design
- Visual arts

If you've never done so before, design a couple of sites. See how they turn out. Learn from your experiences. Learn to design by designing. Get a big picture of the organization that you're helping, what it's all about, where it's going, why it exists, its mission, and its vision. Create a flowchart of that information. This will help you more than all kinds of technical skills as you try to communicate who the organization is.

How to Get Started
Volunteer your services to small churches, non-profit organizations, and community agencies.

7 WEB RADIO STATION OWNER

Imagine your own radio station listened to by thousands of people all over the world on a daily basis! It's possible. Start your own Internet radio station, with your own message, music, and style. Tens of thousands of web stations already exist, and that number is expanding astronomically.

Currently, the only way to listen to Internet radio is via an online computer connection. Of course, that isn't a bad way to stay in touch with the world. But Internet radio is about to become a lot more accessible. It's likely that in the very near future, Internet radio receivers will be an option in new cars. Portable Internet radios will follow. When that happens, a revolution with be officially underway in the radio business. Your homegrown station may be in competition with other content "out there" on the huge World Wide Web.

GIFTS/SKILLS/EXPERIENCES

- Technical ability
- Creativity
- Love for people
- Background in radio or television

Significant discussion is occurring about web radio stations paying music royalties. But even if courts ultimately decide that these stations should pay royalties, web radio will simply turn toward a talk format and an emphasis on original music. Both formats lend themselves to Christian radio.

Come up with an easy-to-remember name (URL or web address) for your station and you'll attract more listeners.

How to Get Started

For more information on Internet radio, track down the informative book *Web Radio—Radio Production for Internet Streaming* by Chris Priestman (Focal Press, 2002).

You'll attract an audience by connecting on the web with strangers (aim to land links on complementary sites and research how to come up on search engines) and through word of mouth. Print cards with your web address and give them to people willing to listen to you carry on for a minute or two about your pet project!

8 COMPUTER SKILLS INSTRUCTOR

Specialize in two or three areas of popular software and become thoroughly familiar and fluent with those. Consider mastering

Gifts/Skills/Experiences

- Patience
- Presentation abilities
- Speaking
- Teaching
- Technical ability
- Business

Microsoft Works and training others in it. This software package covers the basics of word processing, spreadsheets, and presentations.

Put together versions of your presentation appropriate for children, highschoolers, beginning adult users, and more advanced adult users. Because most people are pretty intuitive, gear your presentations to the quicker instead of the slower ones. Aim for the top 10 percent of your participants; they'll "get it" and help the slower ones along. Ideally, you'll make your presentation in a classroom setting with a projection of your screen for the class to see. Participants also need computers of their own to use.

How to Get Started
Place flyers at computer stores and put announcements or ads in community giveaway newspapers.

9 WEBSITE TRANSLATOR

People from all corners of the world view the Internet's most popular websites. The best sites are accessible in multiple languages—the most common being English, Spanish, French, German, and Mandarin.

Gifts/Skills/Experiences

- Second language ability
- Patience
- Foreign language teaching
- Technical ability
- Website management

While you can purchase software to translate web content from one language to another, the result is usually rough and inaccurate. I (Janie) know from experience.

Many people are more fluent reading and writing a second language than they are speaking it. Perhaps your ministry will involve translating a site or checking what's already been done for accuracy.

Finally, even if you don't do the actual translation work, you can serve as the organizer of a large project.

How to Get Started
Offer your services to computer users' groups. Go online to your favorite Christian sites, hit the "contact" link, and see if they're interested in translations for international constituents.

10 COMPUTER PURCHASE CONSULTANT

Buying a computer can be a mystifying experience for nearly anyone. You need to possess a specialized technical vocabulary suited specifically for the computer world in order to be totally successful.

We've met very few well-informed computer sales personnel. For the most part, they're neophytes who know just a little bit more than we do—but perhaps just enough to be dangerous! Usually, they just know more computer "lingo."

So most of us are forced to depend on a kind friend who has a little extra time in his or her schedule to help us make our purchases. That's not the best way to do things. A much better approach is to have a professional computer shopper help us.

With this ministry, you'll help others pick out the right computer to buy. Don't just recommend the kind of computer you'd like to have. Help them assemble the right computer hardware and perhaps software choices for their needs and goals.

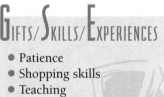

Gifts/Skills/Experiences

- Patience
- Shopping skills
- Teaching
- Computer skills
- Technical ability

How to Get Started
Place flyers or business cards in computer stores. Make small churches and non-profit organizations aware of your services.

11 INFORMATION TECHNOLOGY (IT) COORDINATOR

If you have experience in the IT world, you could take care of all the computer needs of a small but growing church or a small business or non-profit. As needs increase, you can put together a plan and a team of people that you oversee rather than doing all the work yourself.

You might take on the all-important task of helping a congregation, non-profit, or business go digital. Many smaller organizations still have equipment that needs to be updated to the digital world. Set up an operation that includes an e-mail server and a local

Gifts/Skills/Experiences

- Patience
- People skills
- Information technology
- Information processing

area network (LAN) to facilitate communication both internally and externally.

How to Get Started

Find a non-profit, business, or church that has a vision you're excited about. Many are probably ready to update their networks and systems and have been waiting for someone who can help them avoid expensive mistakes.

12 AIRPLANE PILOT (FOR CHURCHES AND MISSIONS ORGANIZATIONS)

If you're a pilot, put your experience to good use. You can offer to fly church leaders to regional events for the cost of fuel. Or become a pilot for a missionary organization.

Because I (Steve) speak around the country a lot, I know from experience how much more convenient it is to fly on a private plane than to fly on a commercial one. If you operate from a convenient local airport, you could help pastors and organization executives get to where they need to be, saving them time and money.

For more information on aviation ministries, connect with Mission Aviation Fellowship at www.maf.org or www.pmafms.org. Many major aviation mission sites can be found through a web search engine.

How to Get Started
Start by connecting with www.finishers.org to get your foot in the door with several agencies that can inform you of their requirements for pilots.

GIFTS/SKILLS/EXPERIENCES
- Love for people
- Patience
- Eye for details
- Willingness to serve to the utmost
- Pilot's license

13 HABITAT FOR HUMANITY WORKER

Habitat for Humanity is one of the finest volunteer organizations in the world. Branches exist in most communities in the United States. Habitat's philosophy is more about giving people a hand up than giving them a handout. They require new homeowners to assist in the construction of their homes and in other homes in the community. They also offer low-interest loans.

GIFTS/SKILLS/EXPERIENCES
- Recruiting
- Organizational thinking
- Problem solving
- Nursing
- Construction
- Business administration

To work with Habitat, you can have about any skill level and be useful. Of course, you'll be welcomed if you have construction experience and skills, but even people without them can help. In the Habitat organization, significant behind-the-scenes work begins prior to the construction of a home, and volunteers are also needed to manage the work while the construction is taking place.

Volunteer positions include volunteer orientation coordinator, construction site leadership, administrative support, and more.

How to Get Started
Contact your local Habitat office; if you can't locate a local affiliate, log on to www.habitat.org.

14 SMALL-GROUPS STARTER

Small-group ministries are common in churches now. Yet there aren't always enough small groups to meet the needs of the adult population of these churches.

One of the keys to a successful small-groups ministry is the capacity to continually start new groups. If you have a passion for the discipleship opportunities small groups offer, you can become a small-groups "launcher." If you have an entrepreneurial personality, you may do particularly well at this ministry.

GIFTS/SKILLS/EXPERIENCES

- Recruiting
- Vision-casting ability
- Teaching
- Leadership

The process of starting small groups seems to be difficult and mystifying. But that doesn't need to be the case. For a great starting point with a lot of pertinent information, read *Nine Keys to Effective Small Group Leadership: How Lay Leaders Can Establish Dynamic & Healthy Cells, Classes or Teams* by Carl George (Kingdom Publishing, 2001).

How to Get Started
After thoroughly studying Carl George's book, contact your pastor with your idea. Ask if you can start new groups and turn them over to existing and developing leaders.

15 SMALL-GROUPS COACH

In most churches, the role of the small-groups coach (the person who oversees several small-group leaders) is of supreme importance. He or she encourages the forward progress of the small-group leaders.

Gifts/Skills/Experiences

- Love for people
- Vision-casting ability
- Leadership
- Speaking skills
- Marketing

Finding and maintaining great coaches is always the most difficult part of a small-groups system—*always*. Carl George explains the role further in his book *Prepare Your Church for the Future* (Chosen Books, 1991). The basic idea is to provide encouragement and support for small-group leaders. George recommends one coach for every five to ten small-group leaders. More than ten leaders is beyond the "span of care" that one person can realistically provide. He also recommends that all leaders and coaches constantly train apprentices to replace themselves. This not only encourages mentoring relationships, but also lays a grid for future growth.

As a small-groups coach, you can be a key to the success of your congregation's small groups. As you begin and develop a great system of coaches, you'll end up with a great system of small groups—it's about that simple.

How to Get Started
Contact your pastor with your vision and desire to serve in your church's small-groups program.

16 BAPTISM DIRECTOR

This is more than getting people wet! It's counseling new believers on their journeys forward in discipleship. It's helping them deal with issues connected with following Jesus as Lord and all the implications connected with that decision.

If you've been a Christian for a few years, you know how far-reaching the implications are when someone decides to follow Christ. As baptism director, you commit to praying for people and to getting involved in their lives. If your church allows it, consider having people who played a part in the new believer's salvation participate in the baptism. You can take photos or videos, and hand out

GIFTS/SKILLS/EXPERIENCES

- Teaching
- Patience
- Love for people
- Leadership

certificates. You can make sure to communicate your church's "dress code" and provide a lot of towels for the baptized.

Spend one-to-one time with new believers before the baptism service to make sure they understand what they're committing to.

You might also assemble a baptism packet for new believers. Include a teaching tape that covers all the bases on your church's view of baptism. Offer a several-week, in-depth class on discipleship issues raised by baptism: new life in Christ, repentance, walking in the Spirit, and so on.

How to Get Started

Contact your pastor with your vision for beginning this ministry. Show him or her this book and the quick overview of baptism ministry written here.

17 NEW-BELIEVER DIRECTOR/COACH

When we were interning at a growing church in West Los Angeles in the early 1980s, one of the first assignments Steve got was to teach the new believers' class. The eight-week curriculum included prayer, how to study the Bible, baptism, new life, and worship. The class culminated with a baptism celebration at Lifeguard Station No. 15 at Santa Monica Beach. A lot of people were coming to Christ on a weekly basis, so the church had a significant need for a director of new believers.

You don't have to be an expert on all matters of faith and doctrine to be effective in coaching new followers of Jesus. Just be sure to cover the basic topics:

- How to study the Bible
- Prayer
- Fellowship
- New birth in Christ
- Baptism
- Worship

If you can't answer all the questions, simply let participants know that you'll get answers. Many books discuss how to grow systematically in Christ.

If you want to see more new believers at your church, encourage your pastor to give more opportunities for people to respond to Christ during your worship services. Pray, asking God specifically to bring people to Christ at your church. He loves to answer that prayer! Get others to pray that with you. The excitement will spread!

Gifts/Skills/Experiences

- Teaching
- Leadership
- Management

How to Get Started

Contact your pastor with your vision for this ministry and your availability. Briefly outline what approaches you might use to teach on the subjects listed previously.

18 NEWCOMER DIRECTOR

Growing churches sometimes have more new people than they know what to do with. Of course, other churches long to have that problem. By becoming a newcomer director, you can help stimulate church growth where it's been lacking.

Churches grow when newcomers feel well cared for. When people visit a new church and feel welcomed, that's where they're likely to stay. If they feel they're simply an afterthought, they're not likely to return.

Establish a class for newcomers—a series where new folks coming into your church can learn about your church—something akin to "Church 101, 201, and 301." Cover the mission of your church, its history, who the church is (its values), where it's going, and how they can get involved.

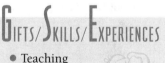

Gifts/Skills/Experiences

- Teaching
- Leadership
- Public speaking

Set up a system for following up on newcomers to your church. Your efforts will pay off in huge dividends. For a complete and detailed treatment of how to put together a follow-up system for your church, see my book *The Perfectly Imperfect Church* (Group Publishing, 2002).

How to Get Started

Talk with your pastor about your vision for this ministry.

19 CHURCH-PLANTING COACH

Church planting is one of the most effective and powerful means of doing evangelism. And it's not necessary for you to have planted a church to help coach church planters.

Church-growth expert Peter Wagner says the ideal church planter is a combination of someone who grew up on a farm (innovative) and who used to sell insurance (a stick-to-it attitude). Are

GIFTS/SKILLS/EXPERIENCES

- Administration
- Evangelism
- Sales
- Insurance
- Multi-level marketing

you someone like this who can lead others? If you have a background in entrepreneurial things in the business world, this ministry might fit you well.

Coaching training is available with Church Resource Ministries at their training events; for more information, log onto www.crmnet.org.

How to Get Started
Contact your denomination or fellowship to learn about training opportunities for becoming a church-planting coach.

20 DIRECTOR OF MINISTRY TO PEOPLE IN NEED

God is passionately in love with the least, the lost, and the lonely. According to the Scriptures, these are even some of his favorite

GIFTS/SKILLS/EXPERIENCES

- Mercy
- Compassion
- Evangelism
- Hospitality
- Teaching
- Social work
- Nursing

people. "The poor you will always have with you" is a promise from Jesus to the church (see Mark 14:17). That's a promise of perpetual employment.

Set up a system or coordinate and expand existing programs to get the people of your congregation outside the boundaries of the church and into the presence of the poor and needy. Direct people to ministry opportunities with the needy in your commu-

nity. As they serve, the people of your church will be blessed beyond words and in indescribable ways. Also, serve as a cheerleader and administrator for the cause of the needy at your church.

For specific ideas about how to get going in ministering to the needy, pick up a copy of our book *101 Ways to Help People in Need* (NavPress, 2002).

How to Get Started
You can work with your own church or work in tandem with several churches to establish ministries to the needy. Also, don't overlook existing agencies in your community where workers from your congregation can serve.

21 ALPHA COURSE DIRECTOR/CONSULTANT

MINISTRY

Alpha is a ministry focused on introducing those who are seekers or new to the faith to the foundational truths of Christianity. We have seen it used at churches around the world and have found that when people apply the principles, their faith grows. This international ministry has been phenomenally successful in much of the developed world. It helps people clarify their faith in Christ and, in many cases, come to an initial faith in Christ.

At Vineyard Community Church in Cincinnati, we've had great success employing the Alpha course, even though we're not a program-driven church. People respond to the information and grow in their faith.

As the course director, you may want to teach the materials yourself instead of using the videotaped sessions. If you have communication gifts and are comfortable in front of a crowd, this is a great option.

Once you become proficient with the Alpha course material, you can become a consultant for area churches that are just starting Alpha programs.

GIFTS/SKILLS/EXPERIENCES

- Administration
- Evangelism
- Discipleship
- Comfort with the gifts of the Holy Spirit
- Leadership
- Mercy
- Teaching
- Nursing
- Management
- Human resources

How to Get Started
Check out the organization at www.alphausa.org. Then meet with your pastor and share your vision for starting an Alpha course at your church.

22 DOOR-TO-DOOR INTERCESSOR

Anyone who says, "God, I'm available," can do this ministry. Perhaps like no other idea in this book, this ministry will generate a lot of "war stories." You may find this idea too intimidating if you go out by yourself. To be more effective, you'll need to find a partner to take away some of the jitters.

GIFTS/SKILLS/EXPERIENCES

- Boldness
- Diligence
- Intercession
- Sales
- Counseling

Keep a journal of prayer requests alongside prayer answers for your encouragement.

You can expand your outreach to prayer-request boxes that are placed in public places like convenience stores. Leave a pad that asks for requests, name (optional), and a description of the person's needs. On the pad, clearly state your intention to "just pray"; you're not looking to sell anything or proselytize.

How to Get Started
Knock on the doors of strangers and simply ask, "Is there anything I (we) can pray about for you?" Take the direct approach!

23 PRAYER WARRIOR

These ideas for prayer ministry differ from the "cold turkey" approach of praying door to door. But they still involve being available to God and to others in need of spiritual care.

Some versions of this ministry you might consider:

- *Prayerwalking.* Split your community into sections and then pray as you walk through it systematically. Keep a record of your discoveries. Share those with other intercessors. Read the book *Prayerwalking* by Steve Hawthorne and Graham Kendrick (Creation House, 1993).
- *Prayer flyers.* You've seen those public boards in grocery and drugstores announcing items for sale or childcare availability. Put up your own cards: "Need Prayer?" Then offer your phone number or e-mail address. Again, be clear that you're not selling anything or collecting names. Your main concern is getting people's prayer requests.

• *Ads.* If you want to take this a step further, consider taking out a Yellow Pages ad next to the palm readers and psychics along the same lines: "Need Prayer?" Once you place an ad like this, you will get calls for

- Patience
- Prayer
- Counseling

years from desperate people seeking spiritual help, so be ready! You could have a phone line with a message machine to take only these calls; additionally, you could offer an e-mail address to receive requests.

IN ACTION: One friend goes to the beach boardwalk in Venice, California—a place that attracts a lot of interesting people on weekends. He sets up a "Free Prayer" table next to psychics, channelers, and other mystics. For several hours, he's busy nonstop, praying for people who are spiritually hungry.

One woman in our church became a Christian in her mid-fifties and began to learn to pray by making herself available to pray for others. Now she is busy most of each week praying for a steady stream of others in need. Wherever she goes, people seek her out for the prayer she offers.

24 HOSPITAL VISITOR

People who are stuck in the hospital—especially for extended stays—need encouragement and spiritual care. I (Steve) know from several long hospital stays how discouraging and depressing hospitals can be.

For some people, a hospital's surroundings decrease their faith. But if you're someone whose faith is activated by the smells, sights, and sounds of a hospital environment, then perhaps this ministry is for you.

Some of the best people for this kind of ministry are those who've had their own extended stays in the hospital. They know the loneliness firsthand.

Perhaps you're called to be a chaplain or a chaplain's assistant. While some hospitals require a seminary degree to join the staff as a chaplain, if returning to school isn't something you're interested in, you can become a chaplain's assistant. Some hospitals have a chaplain's apprenticeship program for non-degreed people.

Contact the chaplains at several hospitals with your availability, willingness, and eagerness to serve. You can work at more than one hospital. Veteran's hospitals will be especially open to this ministry; a lot of lonely and forgotten people end up at these places long-term.

Gifts/Skills/Experiences

- Compassion
- Listening
- Personal prayer
- Counseling
- Pastoral care

A gifted person who simply cares about the spiritual well-being of his or her patients goes a long way toward lifting their spirits. What counts most in this area is consistency—showing up day after day to say hello, listen, and see if you can pray for anything.

How to Get Started
Set up interviews with several local hospital chaplains to get to know them and to express your interest in helping meet the spiritual needs of patients.

25 WEDDING MINISTER/COORDINATOR

In larger churches, it's increasingly common for designated pastors or volunteer pastors to be specially trained to perform weddings. Often this works great because the couples getting married receive excellent attention from the "marrying" pastor. They certainly receive more personal care from this specialist than an overworked staff pastor or the pastor of a small church could provide.

Gifts/Skills/Experiences

- Patience
- Listening
- Public speaking
- Human resources
- Teaching

Even in a smaller church, people assume that the do-it-all lone pastor will officiate at all wedding ceremonies. But even in this setting, a specialist—a volunteer pastor who simply deals with weddings—can probably do a better job. While this concept might take some adjustments in people's thinking, it can open up a whole new range of ministry opportunities for lay people.

People performing weddings will need to be licensed by their local church board of elders or trustees (depending on how their church leadership is set up).

For a good resource on wedding ceremonies, check out the

book *Weddings from the Heart: Contemporary and Traditional Ceremonies for an Unforgettable Wedding* by Daphne Rose Kingsma (Conari Press, 1995).

How to Get Started
Approach your pastor or pastoral staff with this idea. Or, if you're truly bold, take out an ad in the Yellow Pages. This ministry will put you in touch with a lot of people at vulnerable points in their lives who are very open to receiving spiritual counsel.

26 FUNERAL MINISTER

No matter what the circumstances are, when a family member dies, the surviving family members always face crises and a variety of needs. As with wedding ministers, volunteer funeral ministers often do as good a job—or better—than professional pastors. They have the ability to give heart and soul to the task of caregiving. During times of grief, families need nearly 24/7 care, something a pastor who is running a church just can't provide.

This job requires skills at speaking, pastoral care, listening—and great patience. You'll need a ministry license and a cell phone for availability. Put together a team of volunteers who can spring into action with practical helps when a death occurs—food, flowers, listening, and communicating "We love you. We are here for you." This care needs to take place not only at the time of the death, but also as a follow-up on the family in the weeks afterward.

GIFTS/SKILLS/EXPERIENCES
- Patience
- Listening
- Human resources
- Counseling
- Pastoral care

Learn from a veteran pastor how to do funeral ceremonies. Ask a number of pastors how they conduct funerals, what they say in the service and to grieving people one on one, and what seems to be effective in different settings in terms of a message.

I recommend you pick up a copy of the *Book of Common Prayer* (available at Christian bookstores or on the Internet). A number of classic funeral service liturgies are most helpful. Many provide recommended Scripture verses appropriate for funerals.

When I do funeral services, I often encourage friends and family to speak briefly about the deceased. We also may put together a video presentation of photos and video clips to capture the person's life. In fact, putting together such video histories could be a ministry on its own.

How to Get Started
Contact several funeral homes (with your business cards) to make them aware of your availability. Also, connect with your pastor and suggest that you have an idea that could give him or her more time to devote to other areas.

27 PASTOR ON CALL

Pastoral care—the not-always-so-simple task of caring for a local congregation—seems to be a full-time job and then some. As the pastor of a number of churches in various states of growth, I (Steve) know from experience the sometimes unrealistic expectations placed on pastors. To counteract these, consider putting together a system of oversight care called Pastor on Call.

GIFTS/SKILLS/EXPERIENCES

- Listening
- Pastoral care

The idea is to offer twenty-four-hour emergency pastoral care. Each pastor and volunteer takes a twenty-four-hour shift. It takes twelve to fourteen people to make this system work and to prevent burnout. Pastors and volunteers each take a shift, once every couple of weeks.

You'll need pagers so that when people call in for help, you'll receive notice. You'll also need cell phones to return calls at all hours and locations (set the standard of fifteen minutes for a return call). You'll also need to be licensed for ministry in your state, with a wallet-sized version of your license to show at hospitals and emergency sites.

Before you begin this program, ask group members to meet to assemble a notebook of local resources that the Pastor on Call can point people to. Many callers will be asking for assistance with needs beyond the scope of your church's resources. But you can direct them to a social service agency that can give them adequate help in their time of need. Include phone numbers for emergency housing, low-income medical clinics, transportation, and so on.

How to Get Started
Once you gather your group of pastors and volunteers, publish the emergency number in your bulletins and newsletters. List the

number on the church's after-hours recording, as well as on your church website.

28 MISSIONARY

Not every mission group will be equally open to the concept of middle-aged and older mission personnel, but the wise ones will be. As they consider your life skills and experiences, they'll realize that you have a tremendous amount to offer.

Unless you have a highly developed skill that's in short supply, you may need to receive specific training to get you in the door on the mission field. However, areas such as elementary school teaching, English as a second language, science, or mathematics are good specialties you might already have.

A number of missions organizations are open to middle-aged volunteers. You just need to find the right organization for you. A fantastic resource that lists many organizations is www.finishers.org. They specialize in helping people find a place to reinvest their lives in ministry. This group, an extension of Campus Crusade for Christ, has hundreds of specific opportunities available in dozens of countries. If you're interested in a full-time mission opportunity, check out their website.

GIFTS/SKILLS/EXPERIENCES

- Serving
- Evangelism
- Teaching
- Missionary orientation
- A variety of backgrounds, depending on the field work you're pursuing

How to Get Started

Visiting the website www.finishers.org is a great place to begin. Also, check with your denomination or fellowship's local or national missions board.

29 MISSIONARY ENCOURAGER

You don't necessarily need mission field experience to bring strength and encouragement to missionaries.

Missionaries are vastly underencouraged. These people often give and give with little in return. Serving on the mission field can make for a lonely life. Missionaries need a boost to lift their spirits on a regular basis. Often they're on their own most of the time.

The human heart desperately needs acceptance, affirmation, and assistance. Acceptance means loving them exactly as they are and where they are. Affirmation means offering them friendship without conditions. And assistance means offering help with practical matters in their lives. These are the things that an encourager can offer missionaries who give their best in distant, lonely, and isolated corners of the world.

GIFTS/SKILLS/EXPERIENCES

- Teaching
- Encouragement
- Listening
- Missions
- Human resources
- Sales
- Nursing

A missionary encourager goes to the mission field or does positive public relations on the home front—or both. If you can travel to the field, bring your spouse, a budding leader, or a team of folks. Find out what items you can bring that will bless the missionaries. Let people in your church participate by giving as well.

Positive public relations on the home front includes relaying stories from the field to people in your church to help meet the missionaries' spiritual or material needs. It also means staying in close contact via e-mail on a regular basis.

How to Get Started
Connect with www.finishers.org for opportunities to encourage missionaries if your church or denomination doesn't have its own missionary connections.

30 SPORTS INSTRUCTOR

Almost all of us participate in some sort of sport now and then. But some people excel at a sport—they're born with a high "sports quotient," allowing them to do sports naturally.

Beyond that, some people have the ability to teach others sports skills. If you're one of these rare people, offering free or low-cost sports instruction can be a great way to interact with your community.

Are you skilled in golf, tennis, swimming, fishing, croquet, basketball, or volleyball? Consider teaching teens or children as well as adults. People will gladly pay to receive instruction in many of these sports, so you shouldn't have any trouble getting a crowd to follow your offer of free instruction. Spend as little or as much time as you want by choosing the number of classes and students. You can do this regularly, seasonally, or as an occasional sports clinic.

Your ability to communicate, motivate, and generate excitement is as important as skill instruction. If you're conducting a sports clinic, bring in motivational speakers and professional athletes to share their testimonies as well as their skills.

Gifts/Skills/Experiences

- Teaching
- Enthusiasm
- Knowledge of the sport
- Fitness coach/enthusiast
- Coaching
- Teacher
- Professional athlete

How to Get Started

Advertise your availability at sports shops that sell products related to your sport, such as at a golf pro shop or a soccer supply store. Local newspapers and church newsletters are also good places to advertise or make announcements.

31 ATHLETICS COACH (FOR STUDENTS)

Work with public and private school children. What a great way to influence young lives!

Some schools are unable to continue sports programs because they can't find adequate coaching staff or they can't afford to hire coaches. Many schools hire coaches who aren't employees; it's not always necessary to be a paid teacher to coach for a school. You can also coach for area leagues, such as youth soccer or Little League baseball.

Think back to your own experience in school. If you played sports, how much influence did your coaches have on you? For many people, their coaches are memorable, positive role models. Coaching, like few other opportunities of influence, presents a powerful way to get involved in the lives of children.

GIFTS/SKILLS/EXPERIENCES

- Teaching
- Communication
- Speaking
- Coaching

How to Get Started

Contact your local school district(s) and your community's parks and recreation department.

32 PROFESSIONAL LISTENER

Most people just need someone to listen. But listening is a lost skill, and very few people do it well. However, you don't have to be a psychologist to give people real emotional help. Listening is a great start.

One reinvestor goes to a coffee shop each day for several hours just to listen to people. He engages them in conversations, but mostly they talk to him. He has a very effective evangelistic ministry there. In the last year alone, he's led dozens of people to Christ. By his calculation, he's directed

GIFTS/SKILLS/EXPERIENCES

- Pastoral care
- Compassion
- Counseling
- Teaching

more than two hundred people to area churches. People naturally connect with him because he listens to them day after day.

You might want to take this ministry a step further and train others how to listen. If you really understand the concepts, teach them in workshop settings for lay people.

How to Get Started

Take a listening-skills class. These are offered in various places by Equipping Ministries International (www.equipmin.org), or in books on the topic. A good starting point is *Listening for Heaven's Sake* by Gary Sweeten and David Ping (Equipping Ministries, 1993).

Contact your church with your desire and willingness to work in this capacity.

33 HOSPITAL WAITING-ROOM ATTENDANT

This is frontline ministry, on-the-spot care for families in crisis. People with emotional crises often have questions about life, the goodness of God, and whether or not God even exists. Those who are stuck in intensive-care waiting rooms are often there for days or weeks at a time.

You can be there to offer help and comfort in simple ways. A glass of water, a pack of gum, a bar of chocolate, and a listening ear can give a little sense of peace to individuals and families in the waiting room. You can also give away worship and music CDs that have comforted you.

Gifts/Skills/Experiences

- Listening
- Pastoral care
- Prayer
- Nursing
- Teaching

How to Get Started
Let area hospital chaplains know of your availability to bring practical care and friendship to people who spend extended time in waiting rooms.

34 CHURCH PLANTER

Perhaps nothing is more exciting in extending the kingdom of God than planting a new congregation. This ministry takes great amounts of energy. A reinvestor can do it when he or she joins a team. This truly exciting ministry is one of the keys to expanding the church.

To read about this topic and all its aspects, study my book *Community of Kindness* (Regal, 2003). Purchase and listen to the tapes *Church Planter's Toolkit* by Robert Logan and Steve Ogne (CPM Publishing, 1991; available at Church Smart Resources, 1-800-253-4276). These materials provide a good and fairly in-depth picture of what church planting is all about.

Gifts/Skills/Experiences

- Evangelism
- Care
- Sales
- Administration

You might also want to be assessed for your spiritual gifts and practical abilities. Many Southern Baptist church associations do assessments for a nominal fee. Contact local district offices for help.

Attend a church planter's "BootCamp." This training weekend focuses on getting ready to plant a church. Get dates on the next and nearest boot camp experience at www.cmtcmultiply.org. This will help you start a comprehensive church-planting plan.

Finally, consider doing an internship or volunteering heavily at a thriving church. You'll learn a lot by being a part of the "behind-the-scenes" action, and it will clarify your vision for your own church plant.

How to Get Started

Contact your denomination or fellowship of churches to see what they're doing with church planting. They may recommend that you pursue a seminary degree before beginning to plant churches. While that can be helpful, it's by no means necessary. Many effective church planters aren't seminary trained.

35 INTERNET MINISTER

The Internet is a growing frontier of all things both good and bad. One of the great things happening on the Internet is the beginning of ministries that function entirely in cyberspace. Start your own!

GIFTS/SKILLS/EXPERIENCES

- Evangelism
- Care
- Pastoral ministry
- Computer skills

The Internet offers numbers of opportunities for ministry that traditional churches don't and can't.

- Availability 24/7
- Anonymity
- Universal, unlimited membership potential

Be ahead of the curve. Pollster and futurist George Barna predicts that before long a large percentage of people will get their spiritual nurturing from the web. Some people can't handle a traditional church for one reason or another. Others may simply be housebound. Though only a handful of Internet ministries exist now, that's going to change in the not-too-distant future. Some existing churches may add virtual groups as an extension of their traditional ministries.

In your ministry, you can include chat rooms, study groups, new believers' classes, and training in various areas, depending on the needs that arise.

How to Get Started

Attract people online through web links, chat rooms, and banner ads that you place at various sites. Banner ads are a great way to advertise; often, they're fairly inexpensive. If you are not trained as a pastor, you will want to work closely with a pastor on this one. Perhaps you have the vision and the Internet savvy on the project and someone else has the pastoral experience to look over your shoulder.

36 FIRE AND POLICE CHAPLAIN

Many local fire and police departments offer chaplaincy programs. If you find one that doesn't, maybe you need to do the legwork of starting one.

Gifts/Skills/Experiences

- Care
- Compassion
- A kind heart
- Counseling
- Human resources
- Nursing

As you become a fixture at local police and fire stations, you'll have increased opportunities to speak into the lives of officers and firefighters. In addition, you'll gain access to people in emergency situations. Many people are open to ministry when their lives are in crisis.

Make sure you carry a pager or a cell phone. Offer to "be there" for comfort or as a spiritual presence when emergencies occur—both for police and fire personnel and for individuals and families affected by an emergency.

How to Get Started
Contact local fire and police departments. You might be surprised how many don't have a chaplain.

37 RV PARK MINISTER

As the population ages, people are moving to where it's warm. While this has always happened, RV parks are growing more rapidly, as baby boomers retire. Tens of thousands of retirees are moving either full or part time to RV parks in southern and western parts of the United States. There they live and die in newly established communities of fellow retirees. This presents a tremendous opportunity to do ministry by starting a ministry in an RV park.

RVers are naturally friendly and easy to get to know because they move around so much. Almost everyone is new all of the time! You might try:

- Holding services in the park's recreation center
- Hosting Bible studies among men's and women's groups
- Starting prayer groups
- Doing servant evangelism projects (read more about that in my book *101 Ways to Reach Your Community*, NavPress, 2001)

- Conducting weddings and funerals
- Ministering to people in the ebbs and flows of their lives

How to Get Started

Contact RV park managers. Locate an RV park that provides adequate facilities to meet in. Also, look for a park large enough to sustain ministry—probably one with one hundred or more spaces. Contact your church or denomination for spiritual covering of this ministry. Sooner or later, you will

Gifts/Skills/Experiences

- Care
- Compassion
- Pastoral skills
- Sales
- Human resources
- Consulting

get into a situation where you need authority beyond yourself. It is a good idea to have this issue settled before you start this ministry.

38 INTERNET EVANGELIST

While this arena for evangelism isn't well developed yet, tremendous opportunities exist to do both evangelism and discipleship to otherwise unreached people via the Internet.

Connect with people through chat rooms. You might start by looking for existing chat rooms that deal with spiritual topics; eventually, you can create your own chat room(s) that deal more specifically with Christian faith.

A good book for a modernistic view of apologetics (discussing your faith with not-yet believers) is *The New Evidence that Demands a Verdict* by Josh McDowell (Nelson Reference, 1999). This book covers virtually every argument a skeptic can raise about life and Christianity from a rational perspective. For a more post-modern approach to apologetics, check out Brian McClaren's *More Ready Than*

Gifts/Skills/Experiences

- Evangelism
- Listening
- Computers

You Realize (Zondervan, 2002). McClaren looks at the changing face of evangelism after the era of the traditional "Four Spiritual Laws."

How to Get Started

Get into existing chat rooms. Purchase banner ads to attract newcomers to join conversations in new chat rooms that you create.

39 ENGLISH AS A SECOND LANGUAGE TEACHER

USA Today reports that a new immigrant arrives in the United States every twenty-nine seconds.[2] Talk about the mission field coming to you! No matter where you live, new people are likely coming into your area. They're all seeking to speak English better, because it will determine to some degree their ability to gain employment and to acclimate to American culture.

As you teach English, you'll have a multitude of opportunities to share your faith in Christ with those you're working with. Many of these people are afraid and insecure in their new surroundings and they're looking for friends, smiling faces, and encouragement.

GIFTS/SKILLS/EXPERIENCES

- Patience
- Teaching
- Spanish

Oxford University Press produces great charts and other materials for teaching English to Spanish-speaking individuals. Some essential materials include the *Basic Oxford Picture Dictionary (English/Spanish)*, wall charts, overhead transparencies, workbooks, teacher's guides, and more. These are all available at www.amazon.com.

One of your biggest hurdles is establishing trust so people will attend. Some immigrants are afraid the government will bother them. Others don't understand how to get the help they might need in other areas of life. Once you establish a relationship through teaching English, you can offer help in many other areas as well.

How to Get Started

Go into Spanish-speaking neighborhoods and knock on doors. Invite people to your classes. Hold classes at a neutral site where people will feel at home.

40 SECRETARIAL SKILLS INSTRUCTOR

Have you ever called a church office and been treated poorly or unprofessionally? If you have the right background, you could be part of the solution.

Think fast: Who's answering the phone at your church right now? Second question: Do they represent your church well?

GIFTS/SKILLS/EXPERIENCES

- Secretarial
- Teaching
- Consulting

Receptionists and secretaries are a church's first line of pastoral care that the outside world comes in contact with. Teach them how to communicate care and respect. A great start is to thoroughly think through the values your church holds and what those answering the phones need to convey as they interact with the public. This is a powerful exercise.

Meet with the pastoral staff of the church and compile a list of desired skills to support the mission of the church. Each church is unique. In addition to phone skills, your teaching program will probably include computer skills in word processing, database management, desktop publishing, accounting software, membership tracking software, and more.

You can also do this ministry with small businesses. They may also be conveying an unfriendly message to their customers through their clerical help.

How to Get Started

While this is an older title, read *Love, Acceptance and Forgiveness* by Jerry Cook (Gospel Light, 1979). This is a great book on the philosophy of ministry. Check www.amazon.com for a used copy.

41 EXERCISE CLASS INSTRUCTOR

Many people pay a personal trainer to help them with exercise routines. But others who need that kind of help can't afford the cost.

Hold classes for people from all walks of life—mothers-to-be, senior adults, busy moms. Offer free or low-cost classes through your church or community center. Use videotapes or other proven exercise programs. Include a warm-up and a cool-down phase, with at least twenty minutes of aerobic exercise. Include some weight-bearing and resistance training. Vary the routine with hand weights, elastic exercise bands, and medicine balls.

As always, recommend that all participants consult with their physicians before starting any exercise program.

So many different exercise options exist that you'll have no problem putting together an exciting program. The main thing is to get people motivated to invest time and energy to get and stay healthy. Offer spiritual principles as encouragement. Take time to share

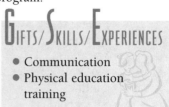

Gifts/Skills/Experiences

• Communication
• Physical education training

prayer needs and pray at the end of your sessions. Distribute a phone list so class members can support each other throughout the week.

How to Get Started
Approach your local church with the idea of starting an exercise class. You can also start one at a local community center. Advertise at church, in community giveaway newspapers, and at local health-food stores.

42 CRAFT CLASS LEADER

Creativity is good for the soul. Whether you're just crafty or truly have some artistic talent, you can open up new worlds to people by encouraging their creative side. Start with a simple project that brings some immediate satisfaction. Break a larger project down into steps and guide people through each step.

Here's your chance to help other reinvestors grow into a more fulfilled and enjoyable time in life. Consider leading a class that makes items to give away at centers for victims of abuse, at nursing homes, or to other people in need. Projects could be seasonal, practical, or just great to look at! Once you choose a project, make sure you have an abundance of supplies on hand, or provide a detailed list of items your students need to purchase.

You'll need a facility where you can teach the crafts. Set up your station in the center of the room so that all your students can watch you and then learn by doing. A church or community center can be a good place to

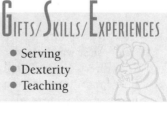

Gifts/Skills/Experiences

• Serving
• Dexterity
• Teaching

hold classes; if you have a large home, that can work as well.

Some of the most popular crafts to consider teaching are:

- Sewing (have everyone bring his or her own machine)
- Painting
- Pottery
- Ceramics
- Macramé
- Sculpting
- Quilting
- Scrapbooking

How to Get Started

Advertise at your church and in local community centers. Also, local AARP chapters and senior centers are great places to connect with people who might want to learn a new hobby.

43 LITERACY WORKER

Millions of adults in the United States are illiterate or barely literate. Considering how easy it is for most people to read once they've received training, this ministry can bring significant satisfaction to both the trainer and those being taught to read.

You may want to start a mentoring literacy program for students. The U.S. government offers grants. To search for these and to find existing literacy programs near you, see www.nifl.gov/lincs.

To get a kit for literacy tutoring, log on to www.literacyvolunteers.org. This site also has frequently asked questions and a lot of success stories to encourage potential teachers. You'll find books and other teaching materials at this site as well.

GIFTS/SKILLS/EXPERIENCES

- Teaching
- Patience

Finally, for places to learn how to teach literacy, log on to www.literacyonline.org.

How to Get Started

The easiest way is to work for an existing agency. Go to www.literacydirectory.org. Simply enter your ZIP Code and you'll likely find opportunities for volunteering within miles of your home. If nothing exists near you, take out an ad in your local newspaper and volunteer to work with those in need of literacy training. Meet at a neutral location (such as a library) for instruction.

44 REINVESTOR COACH

Who directs people going through the big changes in life—from working strictly for a paycheck to working for something more meaningful? You can provide emotional and practical support for groups of reinvestors over cups of coffee.

Give pastoral care to these people, who are at a crossroads in life. They may be ready to go forward, but they need encouragement and clear thinking to lead the way. You can serve them in a profound way.

GIFTS/SKILLS/EXPERIENCES
- Consulting
- Counseling
- Teaching
- Nursing

Distribute copies of this book to those contemplating this kind of significant life change. Challenge them to think through what they love to do, what motivates them, what inspires them. Look to see what feeds their dreams.

Start a support group that meets weekly to look at issues related to the sacrifices of moving into a reinvesting ministry. This group can be of great value as it gets into Bible study, prayer, and emotional support of its members. Share stories and give each other feedback and encouragement, and celebrate attempts to make a difference in the lives of others.

How to Get Started
Advertise your group(s) at church. Once you get started, word-of-mouth connections are also effective.

45 MISSIONS MENTOR

Are you excited about world missions? Extend your enthusiasm to others.

You need a church or churches to work with as well as information to disburse about world missions. Bring in speakers, such as missionaries who've recently been on the mission field.

Put up a map with information about missionaries and their current needs that people can pray for. Communicate the practical needs of missionaries and their encouraging stories through your church's newsletter or a new newsletter specifically devoted to missions.

Gifts/Skills/Experiences

- Public speaking
- Encouragement
- Teaching

One tool that can get people excited about missions is the U.S. Center for World Mission's "Perspectives on the World Christian Movement" course. You might commit to taking the course, and then teach one or more of the sections in area churches. Most people who take this course inevitably get excited about world missions. Many have even been moved to go to the mission field.

How to Get Started

Get more information on "Perspectives on the World Christian Movement" at www.perspectives.org or www.uscwm.org. You might also read the book *Perspectives on the World Christian Movement: A Reader* by Ralph Winter (new edition; Gabriel Resources, 1999). Discuss this idea with your pastor and announce the course in your church's newsletter and worship folders. Connect with other local pastors and offer to teach the course in their churches as well.

46 HOUSEHOLD FINANCIAL COACH

Everyone deals with money. If you're fairly successful at it, you can empower others to be in control of their finances. Teach people to track spending, budget for fixed and discretionary expenses, plan for the future, plan their giving, and use tax advantages.

Gifts/Skills/Experiences

- Teaching
- Compassion
- Mercy
- Accounting
- Finance

Some materials to base your work on: *Good Sense: Transformational Stewardship for Today's Church* by Dick Towner (Zondervan, 2002), and two classics, *Master Your Money* by Ron Blue (Thomas Nelson, 1997), and *Your Money Counts* by Howard Dayton (Tyndale, 1997).

You can offer classes on finances in general from a biblical perspective. And you can offer one-to-one help with people at all stages, from a young couple trying to put their first budget together to a widow needing advice about investments. If you get questions that are over your head (about investments, for example), have your Rolodex ready with references to financial advisors who can help with in-depth analysis and coaching. Choose people who sell a variety of financial products and represent a number of financial institutions.

How to Get Started
Announce your availability in your church's bulletin or newsletter. Advertise classes in the local newspaper. Because money is such a universal topic, people from other churches and unchurched people might want to attend.

47 HOUSEHOLD ETIQUETTE COACH

In our community, whenever local Girl Scouts sponsor an etiquette event, the class fills up quickly and is standing room only. It's hard to believe so many mothers and daughters want to learn about how to properly use forks and spoons.

GIFTS/SKILLS/EXPERIENCES

- Patience
- Girl Scout leadership
- Teaching

The gold standard when it comes to matters of etiquette is still *Emily Post's Etiquette* by Peggy Post (HarperCollins, 1997). Updated for modern times, this source addresses current issues and questions. A secondary source is *Things You Need to Be Told* by the Etiquette Girls (Berkley Publishing Group, 2001). Another tool for teaching is *The Complete Idiot's Guide to Etiquette* by Mary Mitchell and John Corr (Alpha Books, 2000). It includes tons of facts and tidbits about dining, business, correspondence, entertaining, manners, saying the right thing, *faux pas,* and fun games. Armed with these books, you'll have enough information to do a very thorough seminar on current etiquette for virtually every situation.

You could easily charge for this seminar, and people would gladly pay to attend. However, in the spirit of a reinvestor, it would be nice to do this for free just to connect with people who don't yet understand God's love in a personal way. As part of your presentation, explain that you do this as your way of showing them that God loves them profoundly. After saying that, be sure you do a quality job in your presentation!

How to Get Started
Contact local chapters of the Girl Scouts, Camp Fire Girls, and 4-H.

48 NUTRITIONAL COACH

People have great interest in learning how to live healthier, longer, better lives through proper nutrition. So much information exists that it can be a bit intimidating to read on the topic.

If nutrition is something that naturally interests you and you're a walking advertisement for good health, amass files that you can pass on to people in various stages of nutritional need. In addition to diet, you can bridge the concepts to several lines of vitamin, mineral, and nutritional products. Be careful not to come across as self-serving by pushing one line of products that you'll profit from. In fact, true reinvestors who minister in this way would be better off not selling any products.

GIFTS/SKILLS/EXPERIENCES

- Patience
- Compassion
- Research
- Teaching
- In good health

Many people have lived on French fries and Cokes much of their lives, and they're unaware that their bodies have started to break down. But when they become vastly overweight or have constant colds or chronic bronchitis or allergies, they'll begin to wake up to the advantage of diet and exercise. The good news is that it's never too late to start a regimen of good nutritional habits.

Put together a basic healthy-living seminar that you can teach in an evening or a Friday evening and Saturday morning combination. Good books on basic nutrition include one we especially like: *Cancer Battle Plan: Six Strategies for Beating Cancer* by Anne and David Frahm (J. P. Tarcher, 1998). This is both a very practical and an encouraging book on basic nutrition and healthy living.

As you read books and other information, settle in on one or two that you can recommend to people as basic primers on getting started down the path toward healthy living.

How to Get Started
Advertise at local health-food stores and in free community and alternative newspapers. Set up a booth at health fairs. Announce your classes at your church. Once you get started, word-of-mouth networking will take over—those you've helped will tell their friends.

49 LEADERS OF TOMORROW MENTOR

Do you have a special person who spoke into your life at a critical time in your development? Did you have anyone who believed in you enough that you began to believe in yourself? One advantage of being older is that sometimes people think you're wiser and they'll listen to what you have to say. And they'll feel honored that you're interested in their growth. Ask God and your pastor to help you identify people who'd benefit from a mentoring relationship.

GIFTS/SKILLS/EXPERIENCES

- Listening
- Leadership
- Business
- Administration

Spend time regularly listening to, encouraging, and praying with the individuals you mentor. Choose great books to read and discuss together. The investment of time will definitely change both of you. From our experience, whatever amount of time you invest in these people will pay back big dividends to you, your church, and ultimately, the kingdom of God.

While younger generations don't seem to have a hang-up about gender, we still recommend men mentoring men and women mentoring women.

A lot of people benefit from this sort of personal attention: new moms, new believers, newly married people, and people in new careers.

How to Get Started

Let your pastor know you're available to mentor future leaders. Look for people at your church who are already following and growing and learning; seek them out by offering to have coffee.

50 ONE-TO-ONE DISCIPLER

In the same way mentoring can affect lives and help people grow relationally, discipling believers builds a strong foundation of faith for a lifetime. Of course, there are many good books and workbooks you can use. A particularly good resource we have found is "Real Faith." This twenty-four-week study course works great for discipling an individual.

As a reinvestor, you have a large quantity of life experiences to

GIFTS/SKILLS/EXPERIENCES

- Listening
- Teaching
- Pastoral ministry

draw from that can enrich the lives of others. Take the time to share with others who can grow deeper spiritually through your experiences.

How to Get Started

Order Real Faith materials through Life Builders at (612) 869-8790. Their website is www.lifebuildersnet.org. Approach people in your church who are interested in one-on-one discipling relationships. (Again, we suggest you disciple someone of your own gender.)

51 SERVANT EVANGELISM ACTIVIST/COACH

If your church seems too inward-focused, this ministry could be just what it needs.

Servant evangelism—using generosity and acts of love and mercy to show the love of Christ to the world—is growing in popularity in congregations. Many have found that it is—in the most positive sense of the word—addictive. If your congregation has experimented with this approach to outreach, perhaps they're ready to go deeper in this ministry. You could stimulate and cheerlead the rest of the congregation to greater service and outreach.

GIFTS/SKILLS/EXPERIENCES

- Mercy
- Compassion
- Social work

Go out regularly to do projects. Bring people along. Model this kind of ministry to them. This approach to evangelism usually produces a lot of motivational stories. Communicate these stories to the whole congregation to spread the ministry even further. Pass these stories on to your pastor; he or she may well want to include them in sermons as illustrations of God's grace among you.

Read our books *Conspiracy of Kindness* (Servant Books, 1993), *101 Ways to Reach Your Community* (NavPress, 2001), and *101 Ways to Help People in Need* (NavPress, 2002). These are available at www.amazon.com or through the www.servantevangelism.com website.

How to Get Started
You can begin a ministry to the needy by doing any of the ideas in the *101 Ways to Help People in Need* book. One easy project is delivering bags of groceries door to door in depressed areas of town.

52 NEW MOMS' GROUP COACH

New mothers often deal with loneliness, isolation, and a lack of adult conversation. Start groups to provide a place for fellowship and support for these new moms. Each meeting might focus on a different practical topic. Invite guest speakers to share about relevant topics. Incorporate icebreakers (fun and safe questions to get the women talking) as well as deeper group discussion questions. Also include a time for sharing prayer needs and concerns. Consider pairing people up as "prayer partners" for a few months at a time. Give everyone a phone and e-mail list of group members so they can connect with one another in times of need.

If you're someone who has "been there"—even just a step ahead of other moms—you can bring confidence to these women.

Some of the topics moms need instruction on:

- Motherhood as a season in life
- Balanced perspective: juggling marriage and motherhood
- Common ailments of small children
- Time savers for the busy mom
- Nutrition
- Exercising and play with your child
- Home safety
- Establishing positive routines

Gifts/Skills/Experiences

- Nurturing
- Nursing

You might want to check out the website for MOPS (Mothers of Preschoolers; www.gospelcom.net/mops). They've been doing this the longest, and they're especially adept at making these meetings an outreach tool.

How to Get Started
Advertise at your church, at your local Christian bookstore, in your community newspaper, and by putting cards on announcement boards at grocery and drugstores.

53 PROFESSIONAL GRANDPARENT

What's one of the great joys of grandparenting? When it comes to kids, you can love 'em and leave 'em! You can spoil them and send them home! Many parents (including single parents) are in desperate need of a grandparent in the lives of their children.

Why not "adopt" a family in your church or neighborhood and give the parents one night off per month, and maybe even a weekend once per year. Being consistent with one family is a plus. At a time when many families are spread across the country, surrogate grandparents, "aunts," and "uncles" may make all the difference in a family's emotional health and sanity.

This is one way to invest your life in others that isn't a full-time job. We include this idea to encourage you to open your eyes to see what ways you can help lighten the load of people who are already in your life. Don't assume people you already know have all the family support they need.

GIFTS/SKILLS/EXPERIENCES

- Patience with children
- Non-meddling attitude
- Desire to enrich the life of a child

Remember, your role isn't to criticize the children you'll be taking care of. You're there to love them, spoil them a little, encourage them, and be a positive, godly influence. Give them a chance to share what's going on in their lives.

Safety is of utmost importance. You'll need to develop trust before people will allow you to care for their children. Begin by inviting the whole family over for an evening to build bridges.

Suggested safe activities:

- Baseball games
- Amusement parks
- Local community festivals
- Movies
- Ice cream
- Trips to museums
- Interesting historical sites

How to Get Started
Approach people you're already close to at church or in your neighborhood.

54 MARRIAGE ENRICHMENT COACH

Want to make a difference in the world that will affect future generations? Coordinate training and support groups to enrich marriages and families. A great tool to use for establishing a baseline in a marriage is the PREPARE/ENRICH Program. Couples first take an inventory and then attend approximately sixteen hours of training. Some of the topics and exercises:

- Exploring relationship strength and growth areas
- Strengthening communication skills, including assertiveness and active listening
- Resolving conflicts using a ten-step procedure
- Exploring relationship and families-of-origin issues
- Developing a workable budget and financial plan
- Developing personal, couple, and family goals

You'll need a clergy sponsor to oversee the testing. He or she can receive one-day training through www.lifeinnovation.com. More than a million couples have used this training since 1980. And there are more than thirty thousand trained counselors in the United States.

Gifts/Skills/Experiences

- Patience
- Mercy
- Compassion
- Teaching
- Consulting

Once a couple has taken the ENRICH test, the coach discusses areas they need to work on. As a coach, you agree to work on those areas one at a time with the couple, using your own coaching acumen and the coaching materials Life Innovation provides.

An alternative to the ENRICH test is the book *Empowering Couples: Building on Your Strengths* by David Olson and Amy Olson (Life Innovations, Inc., 2000).

How to Get Started

Connect with your pastor and share your desire to get involved with this ministry, and seek to enlist his or her support in becoming a sponsoring church for the ENRICH inventory. Or purchase the *Empowering Couples* book, immerse yourself in the material, and begin to offer help to couples seeking to grow forward together.

55 PREMARITAL SEMINAR LEADER

The format of this ministry is similar to the previous one in that it is based on the Life Innovation test, but couples about to be married take the PREPARE test. (There is also a version of the test for couples with children.) Once the premarital couples receive their test results, experienced leaders provide specific help in areas where the test indicates a lack of compatibility.

Assign a long-married mentoring couple to a premarital couple. At Vineyard Community Church in Cincinnati, where dozens of

GIFTS/SKILLS/EXPERIENCES

- Listening
- Teaching
- Nursing

couples are married each year, four couples oversee this entire ministry. They offer the premarital course multiple times throughout the year in varying formats, such as two hours per week for eight weeks, or four weeks of four hours on Saturdays. Some couples decide not to marry after taking the course, which is probably a good thing.

There's a fee for taking the inventory, but the results are excellent and thorough and well worth the cost. No one has ever complained about this investment!

How to Get Started
Approach your pastor with your desire to become a sponsoring church with this inventory. Prepare for your meeting by visiting the site at www.lifeinnovation.com.

56 DIVORCE RECOVERY SEMINAR PRESENTER

Divorce affects many people, including many within the Christian community. At this critical time of need for support and encouragement, the church often turns its back and sometimes even ostracizes people.

When someone experiences the death of a spouse, he or she often gets meals for a year and sympathetic greetings for a lifetime. People who go through divorce are expected to pull it together within a few weeks or months. The teachers at Vineyard Community Church's homegrown Divorce and Beyond program offer the following advice:

- Divorced people think the church will punish them. Counter this by validating that they are loved by God. God hates divorce, but he certainly loves divorced people.
- Validate the excruciating pain that non-divorced people don't understand.

- Validate that the pain of divorce can even be worse than the death of a spouse.
- Validate the reality of loneliness, isolation, and tears.
- Use humor to help as a coping mechanism.
- Use teams of men and women to lead support groups and discussion groups at seminars. It keeps things balanced.

A one- or two-day seminar followed by supportive small groups can bring healing and turn life around for a divorced person. In most cases, the role of group leader should be filled by a divorced person. A divorced pastor works especially well. Include smiling greeters, icebreakers, and seating at round tables with table hosts to keep the conversation ball rolling. Of course, include plenty of food and coffee.

Invite people through the public records information available at the courthouse (when divorces are made public), as well as newspaper blurbs, church programs, and word of mouth. Recruit divorced volunteers who have

Gifts/Skills/Experiences

- Compassion
- Mercy
- Divorced

been through the seminar to help with table hosting, greeting, snacks, registration, and so on. Our church has offered this seminar twice a year for ten years and continually hears stories of changed lives. The seminar team should meet throughout the year to plan, as well as to hang out and develop a sense of community.

IN ACTION: Joe received an invitation to a Divorce and Beyond seminar after his divorce put him on the list of public records. He came to the seminar and joined the sixteen-week support group that followed. He especially enjoyed the last session, when group members were led to the basement where they received glass plates and bowls (from Goodwill) and a marker. They wrote things on the plates that they wanted to release or grieve the loss of. Then they smashed them against the duct-taped and plastic-covered cement wall! It was a fitting ending to this phase of divorce recovery. Joe became a volunteer with the seminars, led groups, and continued to experience healing and growth. He married his discussion group co-leader two years ago and still serves in this vital ministry.

How to Get Started
Contact your pastor with your idea for ministry. Read *Disappointment with God* by Philip Yancey (Zondervan, 2000)

and/or *Happiness Is a Choice* by Frank Minirth and Paul Meier (Baker Books, 1994).

57 PARENTING MENTOR

Perhaps you've been a parent to several children. You've learned a few lessons (make that *many* lessons!). You need to have successfully gone through your own parenting years to do this ministry. In other words, this one calls for empty-nesters.

Assimilate helpful materials for parents. As you read books and locate magazine articles and material from the Internet, compile these to pass on to the parents you mentor. You might even start your own website to easily disseminate information. One website that has a steady stream of information helpful in reaching out to parents is www.family.org. Sponsored by Focus on the Family, it has new information daily.

GIFTS/SKILLS/EXPERIENCES

- Organizing
- Group-facilitating skills
- Parenting

Put together a seminar for parents. Include an icebreaker to help parents get acquainted. Show some funny video clips to illustrate your points. For example, in *Big Daddy* the foster dad lets the child eat whatever he wants and dress however he wants; *Home Alone* is a classic for sibling interaction; *Father of the Bride* is touching at various points.

In addition to the teaching, include a lengthy discussion time. Ideally, have your participants sit around tables with a volunteer at each. The table leader's job is to make sure each person has a chance to share, to keep the group focused on the topic, and to keep the conversation rolling. It's good to keep the same groups together throughout the course of the seminar. We've found that groups run well for thirteen-week cycles.

Once you have the training aspect of your ministry established, consider branching out to provide counseling for parents in crisis.

How to Get Started
Plan a parenting seminar, but before you give it to current parents, do a trial run with other empty-nesters and ask for their honest feedback. Or collect a team of other empty-nesters who can help present the seminar; give each of them a different topic to present.

58 HOMESCHOOL NETWORK TEACHER

With the rise in popularity of homeschooling, there's a need for specialized teachers. Often, classes such as science work best in groups away from the home setting and taught by someone who's proficient or even has a teaching certification in that area. Other areas where you could serve as a specialized teacher include physical education, art, and the Bible.

Teaching in a classroom setting like this gives you a great atmosphere to impart values and to model your love for the Lord to young, impressionable minds with the full support and involvement of their parents/teachers.

GIFTS/SKILLS/EXPERIENCES

- Speaking
- Teaching

You can do this ministry as a one-time stint, on a weekly basis, or even seasonally. Because a network of parents controls the schedules of the children, you'll typically find flexibility with this sort of teaching.

A great site, which includes a collection of websites homeschoolers can learn from, is www.hsc.org.

How to Get Started
Get in touch with a homeschooling network near you by calling several large churches and asking for the names and phone numbers of homeschooling network leaders in the area.

59 TEACHER OF TEACHERS

Teaching is a fine art. Those who have a gift for teaching and who've mastered the skill should not hold onto secrets they've gleaned along the way. If you've come out of the business or academic world, you've probably picked up significant insights into presentation skills that would be valuable to people who make a lot of presentations.

Develop a seminar based on what you've learned. Put your points on paper in the form of a fill-in-the-blank outline. Also put it all in a PowerPoint outline for presentation purposes.

Offer your services to church workers, small-group leaders, Sunday school teachers, Bible study leaders, church planters, homeschooling parents, pastors, and business leaders. Cover the following areas:

- How to open and close a talk
- How to keep people's interest
- How to make the points you want to make
- How to use stories to illustrate your talk
- How to use visuals for maximum impact
- How to run meetings
- How to best use leadership skills

GIFTS/SKILLS/EXPERIENCES

- Speaking
- Business
- Teaching

How to Get Started
Connect with local churches, home-schooling networks, business groups, chambers of commerce, and so forth.

60 JOB SKILLS TEACHER (TO PEOPLE IN NEED)

If you're from the professional business world and have worked in various office situations, you've probably had a wealth of educational experiences. You can help unskilled men and women develop administrative abilities. Take the skills and knowledge you've accumulated from the world of commerce and develop a curriculum to help jobless people. You'll also be helping people who are underemployed find better employment by increasing their job skills.

Skills to cover:

- Resume writing
- Interviewing
- Office etiquette
- Appropriate work wardrobe
- Phone etiquette
- Word processing
- Mail handling
- Business letters

GIFTS/SKILLS/EXPERIENCES

- Presentation ability
- Familiarity with office systems
- Human resources

Role-play various office scenarios to help train people more effectively.

A comprehensive resource that covers all the possible areas to cover in your training is *The Professional Secretary's Handbook* (Houghton Mifflin, 1995).

How to Get Started
Contact churches that have ministries to people in need. Connect with job-recruiting or temporary placement agencies.

61 SPECIAL SKILLS TEACHER (TO GROUPS)

You may not realize it, but some of the things you do well are skills that others would love to learn how to do. Do you have hidden talents that you haven't stopped to think about? Consider passing on your specialized knowledge in the form of classes. In our busy society, many of the following skills are being phased out. Here's your opportunity to keep a skill alive!

- *Cooking and baking*: Heart healthy; vegetarian; desserts and goodies; on a tight budget; in a time crunch
- *Carpentry*: How to assemble a toolkit; how to use tools; basic home repair and maintenance skills
- *Sewing*: Basic mending; buttons; zipper repair; upholstery
- *Computers*: Windows, Word, e-mail, PowerPoint

GIFTS/SKILLS/EXPERIENCES
- Teaching
- Patience

Don't try to teach everything you know in one course. Make an outline of the steps you'll cover each week. Build into your "curriculum" small successes to create confidence in your students. Create a feedback sheet for them to complete at the end of the course. Ask what they liked the most and least, and leave room for any comments. Learn from your students and make adjustments so you can teach more effectively.

How to Get Started
Attend some similar classes yourself at local businesses that offer them (Home Depot, for example, offers basic carpentry classes). Announce your class in your church bulletin and in community weeklies.

62 IDEA BROKER

Ideas are the most powerful forces in the world. Some people are naturally "idea people." Perhaps you're one of them. Share your

TEACHING

GIFTS/SKILLS/EXPERIENCES

- Communication
- Teaching
- Creativity
- Entrepreneur

giftedness with others. Stimulate them with brainstorming sessions.

Help people put feet to their dreams. Some people dream of writing an article or even a book, but they need someone to help them get organized or someone to believe in them enough to get them started. If you're an encourager, you might have the skills that could help. Or if your experience is in the area of entrepreneurial leadership, this might be a natural fit for you.

You can also help jumpstart other reinvestors into action. Your skill at seeing how things fit together can be invaluable to others. Sit down with people who are interested in making a difference with their lives and with them write out plans for their projects.

How to Get Started

Invite small-business owners in your area out for coffee and offer to help them formulate or solidify their ideas.

PRACTICAL CARE

63 PROFESSIONAL GROCERY SHOPPER

A few decades ago, grocery deliveries were the norm, but that stopped about the time *Dennis the Menace* was canceled on TV. This is a wonderful way to say "I love and care for you" to someone who is homebound. Become a professional delivery service for people stuck indoors because of a physical or psychological impairment.

Other recipients of this service might be families in crisis due to illness, accident, a death in the family, or other temporary situations. Sometimes simple acts of love like this—just picking up groceries or prescriptions—can show God's love in a profound way.

GIFTS/SKILLS/EXPERIENCES

- Serving
- Administration
- Nursing

Create a generic grocery list and organize it in the same order a store is laid out. For example: fruits and vegetables, breads, canned goods, cereals, meats, cleaning supplies, frozen goods, and dairy. (Some stores provide a store map with categories.) Give this list to the people you're serving, and they can mark down items they need along with quantities for you to pick up when you do the shopping. Ask for a spending limit, and stick to it by buying smaller sizes or generic items, if necessary.

How to Get Started
Find out who is in need through your church. People with these kinds of needs can often be located through your church's prayer ministry.

64 COOK

If you have a skill and passion for cooking, convert that into a gift you give away to others. For some people, cooking is a great passion that affords them an opportunity to give away love in a tangible way.

- Start or cook for a free food kitchen
- Cater events for non-profit organizations
- Cook for organizations that serve meals to the needy
- Cook meals for your friends and their spouses
- Cook meals for weddings and funerals

Gifts/Skills/Experiences

- Serving
- Cooking
- Accounting

Become proficient at the art of grilling and you'll be particularly busy in the spring and summer at friends' cookouts. You can find many good instructional books on grilling that cover both techniques and recipes.

You also might use this ministry to cater to work crews putting up Habitat for Humanity homes.

How to Get Started
Make meals in advance and freeze them so they are ready for people in need. If you're doing a catering ministry, put together a team of people to deliver and serve meals and to pray with those who desire it.

65 COLOR AND MAKEUP CONSULTANT

It is amazing how a change in wardrobe colors can make a big difference in the way clothes complement someone's total look. We're not suggesting that you sell products—that would be a compromise of the point of being a reinvestor doing ministry.

You can recommend several lines of products for people to use

Gifts/Skills/Experiences

- Speaking
- Teaching

without being self-serving. Pick up a copy of *Color Me Beautiful* by Carole Jackson (Ballantine Books, 1987; check www.amazon.com for used copies). This uses the remarkable concept that people all have a skin tone or "season" that determines the color of clothing that looks best on them. Even nice and expensive clothes on the wrong tone of skin will look odd if they're not your "season."[3]

Put together a significant array of fabric color swatches to place next to people's skin in order to correctly "diagnose" their seasons.

How to Get Started
Advertise your free seminars at the library, the grocery store, at PTA and AARP meetings, and in local papers.

66 APPLIANCE REPAIR TECHNICIAN

This is a twofold ministry: You can either fix items for people who can't afford to get them fixed (primarily single parents and the elderly), or you can accept broken appliances and fix them to give away to those who are in need.

Of course, you need to have the skills and experience to work on the appliances.

GIFTS/SKILLS/EXPERIENCES
- Patience
- Appliance repair

How to Get Started
Announce through large churches your need to replenish your pile of stoves, refrigerators, microwaves, and washers and dryers needing repair. Connect with those same churches to give the fixed appliances back to the people in need. Broadcast your availability to fix appliances by word of mouth at local churches.

67 POOL CLEANER

Pools are a wonderful commodity for any homeowner, but they do require work to maintain. Why not become the neighborhood pool cleaner and cleaning instructor for free! Do it all to show God's love in a practical way. We

GIFTS/SKILLS/EXPERIENCES
- A left-brained person who is somewhat sensory
- Mechanically inclined

often talk about serving people in need, such as low-income families, single parents, and people with disabilities. But other people need to experience God's love as well.

Pool maintenance is honest, contemplative work—we know from experience. You'll need a set of different pool brushes, hoses, and extendable poles. The people you're serving can supply chemicals and test strips.

Make this ministry part doing the cleaning of the pools and part instructing people in the fine art of pool maintenance. That will engage you in natural and nonthreatening conversations with them.

Go to a pool supply store; ask what the top ten pool repairs are and learn how to do those. Learn the main pool filtering systems and you'll prove invaluable to people with pools. If you can open and shut down a pool for the season, you'll make a tremendous positive impression in any neighborhood. And if you add spas and hot tubs to your expertise, you'll be even more popular.

This is an especially helpful ministry to single parents and those dealing with health crises.

How to Get Started
Put out flyers at your local pool supply store. Go around neighborhoods with pool owners and volunteer your services.

68 LANDSCAPER

This ministry is for people who have a passion for working with soil and who find that doing yardwork is more fulfilling than draining.

Spruce up the neighborhood with flowers, plants, and trees. Make a deal with your neighbors: if they buy the plants, you'll put them in the ground and get them started.

GIFTS/SKILLS/EXPERIENCES

- Serving
- Engineering
- Landscaping

Drive around neighborhoods in your area and look for homes in need of landscape "repair." In a delicate, tactful way, offer to set things in order for the homeowner. It's likely that those in the worst shape have stories behind them—someone's sick, out of work, or elderly. Your willingness to volunteer to help get things back in shape could make a big difference to them.

- Go to hospice centers and group homes and offer to help maintain their grounds. Residents will have something lovely to take their minds off their suffering.
- Go to trailer parks to spruce up the public areas.
- Help freshen up retirement homes.
- Teach landscape design how-tos in low-income neighborhoods. You might be surprised at the interest level in classes you offer there.
- Teach seasonal classes such as shade planting, the best plants for full sun, grass maintenance, weed control, and how to handle pests.

Some specific skills you might need:

- How to trim trees
- How to do edging and trim hedges
- The best ways to plant bulbs

- The best ways to put down mulch
- Lawn cutting and maintenance

How to Get Started

Place flyers on doors to drum up business, then let word of mouth take over. Make single moms, people with disabilities, and the elderly a priority.

69 READER (FOR THE BLIND)

Even with advancements in technology, there's still a need for volunteers to read for the blind. People are needed to read daily newspapers, magazines, mail, and books. Sometimes blind people have a need for someone to read the technical manuals of equipment they're learning to use.

People with sight loss and impairment are incredibly grateful for all the help they receive. This is a highly gratifying ministry. You'll probably need a car to do this ministry, because you'll usually travel to the blind to read to them.

Gifts/Skills/Experiences
- Patience
- Ability to read and speak clearly
- Teaching

Contact the National Federation of the Blind at (410) 659-9314 (www.nfb.org) for further information about volunteering.

How to Get Started

To volunteer, contact your local association for the blind. It can be found in the White Pages of your phone book under "(your city, county, or state) Association for the Blind." Or call the National Federation of the Blind for help locating your local chapter.

70 ANIMAL CARETAKER

Sometimes the fastest way to a person's heart is through his or her pet. When people travel on weekends, you take care of their pets. The idea is to give the animals a lot of quality care plus some "TLC," which they wouldn't get at a pet service.

If you're a real animal lover, this could be the ministry for you.

Consider building space onto your house designated for the care and housing of your animal guests if you're planning to look

GIFTS/SKILLS/EXPERIENCES

- Patience
- Care
- Love for animals
- Nursing

after a number of dogs or cats at a time. You'll also need to research zoning issues and any covenants that apply to your neighborhood.

How to Get Started

Contact local veterinary clinics and let them know your willingness to take in animals over weekends as a ministry. You'll have plenty of takers. Some people will be surprised that you're doing it for free at first. Invite them and their pets to your home so they can see that you're for real and that you have no ulterior motives.

71 GRASS CUTTER/SNOW REMOVER

Nearly anyone can do this ministry. A team of people makes it even more fun. Put together an equipment trailer to make transportation easy. You'll need a decent riding mower, a push mower, a gas-powered trimmer, and a gas-powered grass blower.

GIFTS/SKILLS/EXPERIENCES

- Serving
- Engineering
- Proper equipment

Likewise, purchase a high-quality walk-behind snow blower for the winter or buy a blade for the front of your lawn tractor. This can also be a neighborhood ministry; you'll be the neighborhood hero on snow days when people are in a hurry to get out of their driveways and on to work.

How to Get Started

Put out a few door-to-door flyers in your neighborhood or in the neighborhood where your team plans to serve. Word will quickly spread; focus on single moms, people with disabilities, and the elderly.

72 VOLUNTEER COORDINATOR

After September 11, many non-profit organizations and churches had to cut back on paid staff positions. At the same time, people are hungering for ways they can help make a difference in the lives of others. The answer to both problems is to create more volunteer positions. Churches need to become proficient at developing volunteers if they want to prosper in the coming decades. And, as a large onslaught of the baby boomer workforce enters the reinvestor force in the next few years, it will be necessary to raise up volunteer coordinators to manage these valuable people

A good volunteer program will have many facets. Regular classes with personality and gift inventories will help people get in touch with their strengths and weaknesses, passions, and peeves. Who doesn't want to learn more about themselves? The class should conclude by sharing opportunities at your church and in your community that volunteers can immediately step into.

GIFTS/SKILLS/EXPERIENCES

● Organization
● Administration
● Engineering

Another key to the success of this program is for your church staff and leaders of organizations in your community to create volunteer positions. Challenge these leaders to consider:

- "What can I delegate so that I can be freed up to do more visionary stuff that only I can do?"
- "What am I doing that someone else could do?"
- "Is there a project I can release oversight of?"
- "Is there a project that a volunteer team would enjoy doing?"

The best volunteers are F-A-T. That doesn't mean they're overweight; it means they're Faithful, Available, and Teachable. Look for people who are hungry to get involved. Give them responsibility and ownership.

Treat your volunteers with respect. Help them become experts at what they're doing. Train them and keep them in information loops. Prepare ahead of time so they don't have to wait around for you to clear a space for them and gather supplies after they've arrived. Thank them for coming. Let them know how their help affects the "big picture."

Show appreciation regularly. Thank-you notes, small gifts, and an occasional lunch or coffee with you will go a long way. Public recognition and thanks are one form of pay that volunteers find invaluable. Create a "break room" if you have a lot of volunteers for a big event. Put out snacks and maybe an easel with a message pad to keep people updated.

Volunteers don't work for money; they work for the reward of hanging out with others, serving, and being a part of something greater than themselves. If you affirm and acknowledge those qualities on a regular basis, your volunteers will serve over and over again.

How to Get Started

Connect with the head of a non-profit organization with your vision to serve in this role. A local church might be interested in your services as well.

73 HEALTH-CARE ASSISTANT

With the decreases in insurance coverage for many people comes the increased need for volunteer involvement in health care. Some of the needs:

- Repair of wheelchairs and walkers
- Ramp building and grab-bar installation
- Making beds, washing clothes, and cleaning house for someone who is ill or invalid
- Prescription pickup
- Grocery delivery

Some people want to do this as a job. If you want to be technically trained there are six-month aide training programs and one-year LVN and LPN nursing programs available at community colleges and many hospitals. The turnover rate for aides and LVNs is tremendous because, in most cases, the jobs are thankless and low paying. But to the person receiving the care, it does mean a lot.

GIFTS/SKILLS/EXPERIENCES

- Prayer
- Compassion
- Giving
- Nursing

The need for volunteers and nurses' aides is only going to increase in the coming years as the population ages, as insurance programs become increasingly frugal, and as federal programs receive less funding. All of these present ministry opportunities to help fill the gap.

How to Get Started

Announce your services at church. You can also advertise at medical supply stores and through local senior centers and AARP chapters.

74 FOOD AND CLOTHING MINISTRY LIAISON

With government assistance declining, so is the availability of food for public programs. Yet people in times of crisis still sometimes need to receive food for free, so it's essential that churches and other non-profit organizations collect and distribute food. Many churches and non-profit organizations also have surpluses of fresh food that would go to waste if not delivered directly to people in need.

For more information regarding how to start a food pantry, read that section in our book *101 Ways to Help People in Need* (NavPress, 2002).

Become aware of the free food system that operates in the United States. One organization, Second Harvest (www.secondharvest.org), is a leader in this endeavor. If you're giving away the food with no strings attached, there are a lot of ways you can get the food to distribute. Become an expert with that information. Become known to organizers of the larger food banks in your area and let them know that you can relieve any surpluses they have. Do this by finding smaller ministries in need, smaller local food pantries, homes for unwed mothers and troubled teens, and other shelters.

GIFTS/SKILLS/EXPERIENCES

- Organization
- Serving
- Nursing

IN ACTION: Gordy is a reinvestor who has a ministry of picking up food overruns from various grocery stores, churches, and food banks around town. He then stocks several other food pantries with that overflow. The key to his success is that he's available consistently. Rain or shine, he shows up twice a week. He's able to take items with short shelf lives (such as fresh bread and baked goods) and deliver them to ministries that will use them immediately. Gordy often brings encouragement and joy to other retirees and widowers by having them come along to help.

It doesn't take a tremendous amount of organizing to pull off a significant food ministry like Gordy's. He spends about twelve hours a week doing this. And he blesses hundreds of people.

He does the same with those who have clothing ministries. He takes extra clothes they can't use and delivers them to a local shelter. He has a significant ministry of caring for people in need based completely on the castoff materials of other ministries.

How to Get Started
Contact local food banks and churches, as well as small ministries, such as group homes.

75 POLITICIAN/POLITICAL ACTIVIST

It may sound corny, but some public servants actually change the world! If you have the time to really dedicate yourself to the task, great things could happen. Search your heart. Examine your motives. If you can do it with the right intentions, maybe the political arena is something for you to seriously consider.

Gifts/Skills/Experiences

- Organizational
- Speaking
- Legal
- Teaching

I know a number of wonderfully dedicated Christian politicians who really make a difference in the world. Why not you?

Worth reading to get you started in politics: *Self Matters: Creating Your Life from the Inside Out* by Phil McGraw (Simon & Schuster, 2001), and *Politics for Dummies* by Ann Delaney (John Wiley & Sons, 2002).

How to Get Started

Clarify your vision and your goals for this ministry. Start out at a local level. Gather a team around you to support you emotionally, spiritually, and financially, and to hold you accountable to selfless ideals.

76 WRITER/EDITOR

Do you want to influence a lot of people? If you're good with words, perhaps writing could be in your future.

If you've been a writer or editor, coach others who want to go that direction. Start a monthly writers group for encouragement and motivation. Bring in seasoned authors to share with the group, and leave time for group interaction and processing. Allow members a chance to share their work and get feedback from other members of the group.

It's possible to start writing later in life. I (Steve) didn't publish anything until I was almost forty, but since then I've written dozens of articles in national magazines and have completed eight books.

A book on writing that I've found most helpful is *On Writing Well: The Classic Guide to Writing Nonfiction* by William Zinsser (Harper Resource, 2001). A small book that has proven to be very helpful to me in doing editing is *Elements of Style* by William Strunk (Allyn & Bacon, 1999). Though it's only seventy-eight pages, it's packed with classic insights on writing clearly and well.

How to Get Started
Look into writers' groups in your area by inquiring at area bookstores. Start by writing magazine articles. Write about what you know—an area of expertise. Hopefully, you'll have a seminal idea that appeals to magazine editors.

GIFTS/SKILLS/EXPERIENCES
- Writing
- Editing
- Leadership
- Having been published
- Familiarity with publishing processes

77 INFORMATION RESEARCHER

This ministry is invaluable to pastors, authors, speakers, writers—anyone in need of regular doses of information. You can provide a great service for others who are in a hurry to access information. You might find fulfillment in doing reading and research online and at the library for others.

You need to realize that what you're doing is more than putting together bits of information. Instead, you're assembling a complete picture that will help many others see a message clearly, and in many cases, see great truths that will help them live life more effectively.

GIFTS/SKILLS/EXPERIENCES
- Patience
- Attention to detail
- Librarian
- Engineering research

Consider subscribing to www.lexisnexis.com. There's a fee, but it is the world's largest database service for doing research.

Great gateway sites leading to hundreds of other relevant sites are www.hsc.org (click on "Web Sights"), http://highschoolhub.org, and www.ipl.org (The Internet Public Library). Many public libraries offer access to some subscription sites to cardholders or people who reside in their districts.

How to Get Started
Approach pastors and heads of organizations and associations about your service; they're in a hurry for good information on a frequent basis.

PRACTICAL CARE

78 FOREIGN LANGUAGE INTERPRETER

Many activities that we take for granted aren't available to people whose first language isn't English. Church services, seminars, parenting classes, outreach opportunities, and Bible studies are all out of reach to many of these people.

GIFTS/SKILLS/EXPERIENCES

- Patience
- Proficiency in another language
- Foreign language instruction

More than 10 percent of the U.S. population can speak a second or third language fluently. If you have a second language skill, put it to good use. Perhaps you need to take a refresher course to sharpen your skills before starting your official ministry. But this ministry is one you'll get better at as you practice it.

How to Get Started

Volunteer at your church or at one of the larger congregations in your area. Perhaps they have a foreign language simultaneous translation service that you can help with.

79 HEALTH-CARE PROVIDER (FOR PEOPLE IN NEED)

Not all health care requires a lot of training. We know of people in the San Francisco area who take care of the feet of the homeless. They mostly wash feet and look for infections. Any larger problems are referred to public clinics and local hospitals.

You could also do health-care screening for the needy. Checks of blood pressure, pulse, and respiration, as well as digital temperature taking—all are services that can be provided outside a doctor's office.

GIFTS/SKILLS/EXPERIENCES

- Compassion
- Mercy
- Knowledge of community services for referral
- Nursing
- Medical

Become familiar with what your community already offers. Use this as a means for connecting the homeless with the free care available to them. Often homeless people aren't aware of the services available through churches, government agencies, and non-profit organizations. You don't need to fix everyone's problems. Your function can be directing people where they can receive help.

How to Get Started
Form a compassion team of other reinvestors who will go out to minister to the needy. Offer free health screenings at your church. Announce these in your community newspaper as well as in your church's bulletin and newsletter.

80 FLOWER/VEGETABLE GARDENER

For some people, gardening is more than a sport—it's one of life's great passions!

Brighten up your neighborhood and feed people from the actual fruit of your labors. It's pretty simple, really, to turn your interest into something more extensive.

- In the off-season, grow plants in a greenhouse and get ready for the outdoor growing season.
- Give your product to the poor, the elderly, and low-income families.
- Use your skills to teach people in a needy neighborhood how to plant and care for a community garden.
- Go through your neighborhood in the summer and keep people stocked with watermelons. In the fall, become the giver of great pumpkins.

GIFTS/SKILLS/EXPERIENCES
- Patience
- Science
- Botany/agriculture

How to Get Started
Place flyers on doors or knock on neighborhood doors with your goods. In low-income areas, work through a local community center or agencies that provide other ongoing services (food banks, health clinics, clothing distribution, and so on).

81 MUSIC THERAPIST

Stroke victims, people who've been in accidents, those suffering with cancer—I (Steve) know from the experience of having several extended hospital stays that music lifts the human spirit like no medicine can.

If you're proficient with an instrument or your voice, this might be your niche.

To better understand the theory behind what you're doing, consider taking a course in music therapy at your local university. If you live in a remote area, check the Internet for online courses, or revert to good old correspondence courses from your state university system.

GIFTS/SKILLS/EXPERIENCES

- Compassion
- Listening
- Music
- Performing

Patients who have suffered through any number of ailments show great improvement when exposed to music therapy. Audiences that would be open to this ministry could be found in burn units, hospitals, children's hospitals, hospices, and nursing homes.

How to Get Started
Contact the chaplains at local hospitals. Go to hospice care centers. Check the prayer ministry at your church for people who have needs.

82 MISSIONS COORDINATOR

Perhaps you already have a missions-oriented congregation, but there's always room to grow forward. To greatly increase missions awareness, sponsor the class "Perspectives in World Christian Movement." This will get the ball rolling in a big way with your congregation and will establish great visibility for missions.

GIFTS/SKILLS/EXPERIENCES

- Organization
- Leadership
- Vision
- Missions

Organize teams to go on short-term trips to foreign countries. We prefer to call these trips "serving vacations" instead of short-term missions. That term sounds more positive and contemporary. We plan a lot of fun along the way as we do a lot of good for people in great need.

How to Get Started
For information on "Perspectives on the World Christian Movement," visit www.perspectives.org or www.uscwm.org. Approach the leadership of your church with your vision.

83 CAR MECHANIC

Convert your love for cars into a way to show God's love to your community in a significant way. This is a project that needs a team approach. Some maintenance and repairs you might consider performing:

- Changing oil and oil filters. Find a place that will take used oil for recycling. Assemble a crew of workers to do this on a regular basis if you're working on the same cars.
- Basic tune-ups. With a little training, this can be a fairly simple procedure.
- If you're skilled enough, replace parts such as starters.

Provide your free service expressly for single-parent families and the elderly on a fixed income, and you'll have your hands full.

We recommend you stay away from the heavy-duty overhaul types of fixes. Clarify what you can and can't do. Confine your work to relatively small projects that you feel comfortable with. There will be some projects beyond your capacity, so make your service policy clear.

Gifts/Skills/Experiences

- Mechanical skill
- Not afraid to get dirty
- Engineering
- Automotive

If your church is building an addition or a new facility, consider adding a drive-in auto repair garage. This will open myriad ministry opportunities for years to come.

How to Get Started
Connect with single parents through local churches. Go to Christian bookstores with flyers.

84 TAXI SERVICE PROVIDER

When I was a kid, my mom used to say every once in a while, "What do I look like, some kind of a taxi service?" In the case of this ministry the answer is, "As a matter of fact, yes!"

Are your kids gone from home but you're still driving the mini-van? Do you have a good driving record? Many people's lives would be enriched if you could occasionally provide transportation for them.

As families spread farther apart than ever before, the normal support systems have thinned out as well. For this ministry, you might "adopt" a few people in need. Make yourself and your car available regularly. Decide how many hours a week you're willing to give.

Being part of a transportation team can make a huge difference in the lives of the elderly in your community who just want to stay connected with the outside world. In college I (Steve) regularly drove a small shuttle bus of elderly from a retirement community to the mall. These people were very appreciative.

Gifts/Skills/Experiences

- Patience
- Serving
- Nursing
- Social work
- Good driving record

There are probably already organizations that offer driving services in your city. If no such services exist, start one in association with area churches. Check into insurance issues, split the costs among the sponsoring churches, and you'll be on your way. This is highly rewarding volunteer work.

How to Get Started

Give your name and number (or card) to local doctors to pass on to their elderly patients in need. Put up flyers or your card in medical supply stores and senior community centers, or distribute them at local AARP meetings.

85 ROVING DISASTER-RELIEF WORKER

If it's in your heart to bring practical relief to people who've recently experienced a disaster, consider packing it all up, living out of an RV for part of the year, and traveling to points of need.

People who have experienced a hurricane, tornado, or flood, or who live in run-down houses can benefit from the cavalcade of help on wheels.

A practical construction skill is ideal for this ministry, but it's not essential. Skills in carpentry, electrical work, plumbing, painting, drywall, and framing are especially helpful. But there's also plenty to do for those who can simply clean up, cook, encourage, lead worship, or just see a need and fill it.

Many denominations have a version of this already in place. Assemblies of God USA has the Mission America Placement

Service (MAPS), which offers a program for reinvestors with RVs. Others travel and work for the Salvation Army on the scenes of disasters. For more information on their programs, go to their site at www.salvation-army.org/poverty.

Gifts/Skills/Experiences

- Compassion
- Carpentry
- Electrical
- Plumbing
- Nursing

How to Get Started

Check into your church fellowship or your denomination's ministry to those in need. They may already have a disaster-relief program in place. If not, you can be the one to start it. We recommend you contact MAPS at the Assemblies of God (www.assemblyof-god.org) if you decide to start a new ministry.

86 CLEANING ANGEL

Whether you go solo or get a couple of friends together to form a team of "cleaning angels," you'll be serving in a very practical way. Commit to giving a set number of hours per week.

Put together cleaning kits with the basics: window cleaner, all-purpose cleaner, paper towels, scrub brushes, sponges, toothbrushes, and a razor. Carry it all in a cleaning tray with a handle. Two great resources are *Speed Cleaning* by Jeff Campbell (DTP, 1991) and *The Clean Team* (DTP, 1991). These books give efficiency tips for people who have better things to do with their time. Discover how ideas like "left to right," "top to bottom," and a "shmop" can cut your cleaning time in half.

Gifts/Skills/Experiences

- Patience
- Engineering
- Organization

Once you have formed your team and nailed down a system for cleaning, all you need to do is find some recipients of your work. It might be hard for people to admit they need help, but the offer of a visit from the cleaning angels might be hard to pass up.

Focus on people who can really use the help: new mothers, people whose families are in crisis due to an emergency, people recovering from surgery or an accident, elderly people in need of spring cleaning, or an overworked mom in need of a lift.

The fun of serving together with your team will be a bonding experience.

PRACTICAL CARE

How to Get Started

Leave flyers on doors of people who might want your help, or announce your service through your church's bulletin and newsletter. Check with your church's prayer ministry to learn about people who are facing crises.

87 ROVING MOBILE CAR TECHNICIAN

Fix up a vehicle with equipment commonly used to get a stalled car going: five gallons of gas, jumper cables, and working flasher lights, so that your vehicle is visible when parked on the side of the road.

GIFTS/SKILLS/EXPERIENCES

- Serving
- Organization
- Business

During high-traffic times, drive along the busy roads and freeways looking for stalled vehicles. Use a police scanner and CB radio (tuned to channel 19) to discover where the stranded vehicles are located. You can also contact local police departments and your state's highway patrol division to let them know of your availability.

This is a team project that will take a number of people to finance as well as some means for keeping it going. You'll also need a team of highly dedicated volunteers to keep the whole program running smoothly. In spite of the costs, this can be a high-impact ministry.

How to Get Started

Share your vision with potential financial backers. Assemble a team. Make sure police officers in the jurisdiction you'll be serving are at least aware of your efforts. It may take time for them to realize that you don't have ulterior motives.

88 TELEPHONE CONTACT COORDINATOR

In our time of impersonal contacts, a real human touch is a welcome thing! For members of churches, it can be very reassuring to occasionally receive a call to simply inquire, "How's it going with you lately?"

Every volunteer organization has a high need for someone (or a team of people) to do regular calling for them to let volunteers know of upcoming meetings. A phone call is far more effective than a postcard at connecting with a church's or organization's database of people, even if you only reach an answering machine.

Gifts/Skills/Experiences

You need a relatively pleasant phone voice and the ability to keep going with a high volume of calls. You also need to be able to inspire the troops you're working with—there's a cheerleader aspect with this ministry.

- Patience
- Speaking
- Secretarial
- Multi-level marketing
- Sales

Train your team to make calls short, sweet, and to the point. Quick in, quick out, no one gets hurt! Develop phone scripts that help you accomplish this.

How to Get Started

Approach your church's leadership or contact the leaders of local non-profit organizations with your vision for this ministry.

89 HOME SECRETARIAL WORKER (FOR BUSY PEOPLE)

Are you good at creating workable systems for handling the flow of paper in a home? The mail, newspapers, bills, receipts, and warranties can snowball into a frustrating pile. It's not only a time-waster to be disorganized; it can be costly as well.

Gifts/Skills/Experiences

- Organization
- Good at creating systems
- Secretarial
- Administrative

Use your experience and skills to help someone who is snowed under to dig out. Create a transferable, workable, and adaptable system and then a workshop. Follow up with people who need one-on-one help.

Ideally, you'll be helping busy people to know the fulfillment of being organized.

How to Get Started

Talk to people about their greatest frustrations and needs in this area. Put together a class to address those needs. Teach the class to a group of peers first, and ask for their feedback before you teach it to the moms and others who really need it.

PRACTICAL CARE

90 TAX-FILING HELPER

If you're good with numbers and can understand changes in tax laws, you can help others file their federal and state tax returns. Janie did our taxes for years until they got too complicated.

GIFTS/SKILLS/EXPERIENCES

- Math skills
- Attention to details
- Accounting

Inexperienced taxpayers, people new to the country, and the elderly will all appreciate your help.

There are numbers of books and computer programs on the market to help. Become familiar with a good tax software program. For many people you're helping, this software will be sufficient for their returns. You can choose from several of these, but be sure you can do more than one return with the software you choose.

Because this is a ministry you're likely to repeat year after year, train people you're assisting in the practice of saving receipts and getting organized for you.

With cases that are beyond your level of expertise, refer to tax specialists. Have a number of preparers, accountants, and tax attorneys on file who specialize in various areas.

We recommend the latest version of *Taxes for Dummies* by Eric Tyson and David Silverman (IDG Books).

How to Get Started
Approach apartment managers, particularly in low-income neighborhoods or at senior centers. Set up a table at the apartment clubhouse or meeting area and agree to be there certain hours.

91 PROFESSIONAL ORGANIZER

Some people just don't think (or live) in an organized way. If you're someone who can organize not only yourself but also others, you have an unusual gift that you need to share!

Many areas of a house can use organizing: garages, offices, kitchens. And a lot of people need help in this area. Unfortunately, relatively few people are gifted at being able to help.

If you're really serious about this ministry, you can even receive training to become a professional organizer. Check out www.organized-living.com or www.mnnapo.org for more information about getting started.

Many people will happily receive help in organizing their lives. If they were to purchase this kind of assistance, the price could be substantial—running into thousands of dollars.

Be sure to set up a system the homeowner or homemaker can follow after you've started him or her in the right direction toward clutter-free living.

GIFTS/SKILLS/EXPERIENCES

- Organization
- Communication
- Engineering

How to Get Started
Look for people who are overworked, frazzled, and too busy in life. Who doesn't fit that description anymore?

92 ARTIST

Do you paint, sculpt, throw pots, draw, carve, or even whittle? What do you do with your projects when you're done with them? Many people enjoy watching the creative process. Consider entertaining at parties and church events.

If you can afford to, why not give the art away free of charge to hospitals, hospices, group homes, or senior centers, so that more people can enjoy your work. Your creativity will inspire others.

GIFTS/SKILLS/EXPERIENCES

- Artistic skill
- Creativity
- Art teaching

How to Get Started
All this takes is looking at things from a different viewpoint after your artwork is completed. Try to find places that are devoid of art and would never spend precious resources to buy it. In addition to the ideas above, donate your art to women's shelters, food pantries, or twelve-step meeting halls. If you're already producing works of art, the easy part is finding people who'll appreciate your gift.

93 SHUT-IN MEAL DRIVER

Many people in your community are dependent on someone bringing them one good meal a day to keep them going. Reinvestors we've spoken to report that they form a special bond with those they deliver food to.

Consider establishing a set of "rounds" like a doctor makes.

Gifts/Skills/Experiences

- Patience
- Diligence
- Social work

Adopt a number of seniors and disabled people who are unable to get out and fend for themselves and who might be overlooked by Meals on Wheels (or who are too proud to accept their help). This project falls into the category of James 1:27: "Pure and undefiled religion before God and the Father is this: to visit orphans and widows in their trouble" (NKJV).

You can prepare meals or you can simply be the delivery person. If an organization already provides a delivery system in your community, join forces with them.

How to Get Started

Go to www.projectmeal.org for information about local Meals on Wheels programs. If nothing like this exists in your community, start your own program.

94 COMMUNITY FESTIVAL COORDINATOR

As we've traveled around the country, we've run into a number of churches that have taken a great idea and run with it. They throw a free party for their neighborhood or their entire community in their church parking lot. They don't charge anything and it's all run by volunteers. The purpose is to show God's love in a practical way and to foster a sense of community around their churches.

These events are often planned at least six months in advance and they take tons of volunteers to accomplish. They become a focus on the church's calendar as an outreach event. A lot of people are able to use their gifts and develop leadership skills as they head up various teams supporting the event.

Your festival might include:

- Free food and drinks (hot dogs and orange drink go a long way)
- Games for kids with prizes. Inexpensive prizes can be purchased at dollar stores or online at www.orientaltrading.com.
- Helium balloons

- Health screenings
- Free bicycle repair
- Dunking booths
- Fire and police department involvement (kids love to see fire trucks)
- Entertainment by live musicians (don't forget something for kids)
- Door prizes donated by community businesses (we've given away bicycles, TVs, and radios)

GIFTS/SKILLS/EXPERIENCES

- Organization
- Ability to motivate volunteers
- Detail orientation
- Leadership
- Business administration
- Event planning

If you don't have live music, create a fun environment by playing upbeat music on the PA system.

How to Get Started
Start small. Begin with a part of the festival for just an hour or two. Let it grow year after year.

95 SCHOOL ASSISTANT

Do you have a desire to influence students on a daily basis? Many people find meaningful work in the public school system. Volunteer positions are plentiful, and part-time and full-time jobs offer other benefits in addition to a paycheck. Nights, weekends, holidays, and summer vacations off are a great job plus, especially for those with children still in school. Possible positions:

GIFTS/SKILLS/EXPERIENCES

- Love for kids
- Patience
- Friendliness
- Outgoing
- Teaching

- Nurse/nurse's assistant
- Teaching assistant
- Office assistant
- Administrative assistant
- Food services worker
- Hall monitor

None of these positions requires a college degree, and often you don't need prior experience either. There are daily opportunities to

PRACTICAL CARE

offer smiles, hugs, encouragement, and care to both students and teachers. These positions are less demanding than teaching and offer just as much opportunity for influencing lives for good!

How to Get Started
Contact your local school district or check classified ads for available positions.

96 VIDEOGRAPHER

Do you have an eye for visual details? Use your video equipment and skills to bless families or to help churches and ministries.

Invest in a decent camera. You may want to spend a little more and go digital so you can use editing software on your personal computer. Because you have many choices for both cameras and software that get better and cheaper all the time, we hesitate to recommend particular products. Do some research, and you'll find what suits your needs. Call people who do a similar ministry (at a church, for example) to get ideas of the latest and best equipment.

GIFTS/SKILLS/EXPERIENCES

- Eye for details
- Precision with equipment
- Art instruction or direction
- Engineering

Last, you will need a computer to edit your digital tape. In recent years, the price has gone down dramatically for a dedicated editing computer.

Another idea for this kind of ministry is to capture significant events on video for posterity. You'll be a hero for making family memories. Weddings, birthdays, anniversaries, and graduations are all events that people want to capture.

"A Day in the Life of the Family" is a historical video look at a family. Include clips of the town they live in, favorite restaurants and coffee shops, schools they attend, each person at work or school, and the cars they drive. Have family members share about what makes up their day, what they're excited about, and what they are thankful for. Include their "predictions" for the future for other family members.

Take your cue from TV talk shows. Do "Top 10" lists for viewing at weekend church services. Do a "Survivor's Guide to _____" (fill in the blank with a ministry you want to highlight). Use humor. At Vineyard Community Church, we've done "Survivor" competitions between pastors, "Fear Factor" series between pastors, and pastors looking for a site to build a new church facility. Do a variation of MTV's "Cribs" show and videotape your youth pastor giving a tour of his home and his garage full of cars (Matchbox cars!), his backyard pool (kiddie pool), and—of course—what's in his fridge. You can also record invitations to outreach parties. Write funny poems to get your point across.

For video ideas, see our website www.servantevangelism.com for "Vineyard Memories" videos (click on "online store" then "videos"). We have collections of video clips we've created at our church over the past several years. We use videos regularly in our weekend worship celebrations. And we often show a video during the "transitions"—the time we allow for announcements after worship and before the message. The videos either highlight a coming event or a value of the church, or support a message series we're going through.

In our current multimedia culture, video has a lot more impact than the printed word. This ministry allows you to use it for good!

How to Get Started
Learn by doing! Once you've invested in your equipment, offer your services to people who need to announce events in your church.

FINANCIAL

97 FUND-RAISER

Are you good at mobilizing people? You can provide a great service for local churches or non-profit organizations. Money is tighter than ever in the post–9-11 era. We need to learn how to talk intelligently and passionately about money.

People are willing to give—it's simply a matter of them being approached in the right way by the right person speaking the right words. Some have a gift of making money. They did it in the secular world; now it's time to do it in the church world for a greater cause.

You will need to have excellent people skills to raise money. Work in tandem with the leadership of your church or an organization to raise awareness for needs by putting together communication tools. If you are doing an ongoing project for a church, for example, we recommend they supply you with a gas credit card for your trips (or reimburse you for gas expenses) as well as a budget for taking people out to meals.

GIFTS/SKILLS/EXPERIENCES

- Patience
- Vision
- Communication
- Finance
- Sales

Check out the materials published by Generous Giving at www.generousgiving.org. They specialize in helping people who are seeking to communicate effectively with potential givers. These materials will help you take the intelligent approach to fund-raising and working with givers who give large amounts.

Part of your ministry will be helping pastors become more effective in speaking on the topic of giving. You can direct pastors to a wealth of information (which you can sort through in advance) at pastor Rick Warren's website (www.pastors.com) or at author and pastor John Maxwell's website (www.injoy.com).

Consider expanding your vision—work with several churches and non-profit groups at once!

FINANCIAL

How to Get Started

Connect with area churches and make yourself available to help raise funds. It's important to have a number of conversations with the pastors so you can gain their trust.

98 INSURANCE COMPANY LIAISON

Insurance is a maze for 99 percent of the population—including us! Help bring clarity to the confusion that commonly surrounds the insurance industry.

GIFTS/SKILLS/EXPERIENCES

- Patience
- Serving
- Organizational skills
- Finance
- Insurance
- Research

Many people with medical problems not only face the difficulty of their physical challenges, but also the burden of dealing with insurance companies. Become an advocate for those who don't have the patience or emotional wiring to deal with insurance company representatives.

Once you learn how to deal with insurance companies, it's easier to speak their language.

How to Get Started

Find recipients through word of mouth. Your church's prayer ministry coordinator might know who is battling the complications of a long-term medical ordeal.

99 CAR BUYER (FOR THE BUSY, WIDOWED, OR DIVORCED)

My dad (Steve's) died when I was twelve. I remember my mom, as a single parent, having to go through the traumatic experience of buying her first car alone. In her words, she was "taken." Not knowing the fine art of car buying, she ended up with many extras on the car that she didn't need or want. To make matters worse, she paid practically the sticker price for the vehicle—something almost unheard of in the automobile industry. She didn't have an advocate. She needed someone with a thorough knowledge of cars to come alongside her during the process.

I (Janie) was glad to have help from a reinvestor when purchasing a family van when Steve was recovering from surgery. Greg started and owned a mortgage lending business. We were in a small group together. Greg's presence—along with his confidence and calm demeanor—helped bring the price of the vehicle down sig-nificantly. A couple of small dings and higher than average miles were his leveraging points. He even got the salesman to throw in free car mats!

GIFTS/SKILLS/EXPERIENCES

- Sales
- Teaching
- Administration
- Business
- Car sales
- Auto mechanics
- Purchasing

Experience in car mechanics or automobile sales are a plus in this ministry, but even more important are a desire to get the best deal, confi-dence, and not being afraid of a little conflict. Some have the knack for deal making while others don't. If you're a deal maker for yourself, you can probably get deals for others, too.

Get familiar with www.kbb.com (Kelley Blue Book's site). It will give you up-to-date values for new and used cars of all makes and many years.

How to Get Started

Let your expertise become known by putting an announcement in your bulletin or newsletter at your church. Word of mouth will quickly spread news of the high value of your ministry!

100 HOUSE BUYER

If you have a real estate background, this ministry will be a piece of cake. Use your experience to help people wade through the maze of home sell-ing and buying. Work closely with appraisers and real estate agents. Get familiar with school systems and other variables that define places to live.

GIFTS/SKILLS/EXPERIENCES

- Patience
- A critical eye
- Real estate
- Sales
- Administration

In a large church, this could be a fantastic service to offer people who are afraid of the process of home purchasing and who perhaps are fearful that real estate professionals will take advantage of them. This would be beneficial to single women, first-time home buyers, elderly couples, widowers, and the recently divorced.

A good book to help you work effectively in this is *The Complete Idiot's Guide to Buying & Selling a Home* by Shelley O'Hara (Alpha Books, 2000).

How to Get Started

Advertise via word of mouth through your church; you can also put up announcement cards at grocery and drugstores. Look for "for sale by owner" signs and offer to help them more effectively sell their homes based on your experience in the field.

101 BEST-DEAL RESEARCHER

For some people, finding a deal is like a sport. Others just want to be done with a purchase, no matter what the cost. But for all who've been able to find a great deal, it's something to rejoice in.

The Internet can be a great research tool. Beware that shipping charges may make an item more expensive than one purchased locally. However, you can still get a good idea of the best price for a particular item—and if that item at a store near you is priced in the same ballpark. Two sites worth checking out are www.deal-time.com and www.couponmaker.com.

GIFTS/SKILLS/EXPERIENCES

- Administration
- Sales
- Veteran deal-finder

If you shop at a particular company where you regularly get good deals, ask to be put on their e-mail list for notification of sales. Get familiar with local stores that serve as outlets for overstocked items and sell-offs of last year's products. If you understand the retail cycle—the seasonal turnover of merchandise—you can keep your eyes open for sales and learn to utilize coupons.

You can really help others learn to save money consistently. On a small scale, you can help people make purchases, find deals, and locate good sources. On a larger scale, your can do training on how to find the best deals and save money on everything. Teach these skills in conjunction with classes for newlyweds and women's groups, or financial-planning classes.

How to Get Started

Connect with churches; help them with their purchasing to get the best possible deal. Offer to teach a class to women's and young mothers' groups.

NOTES

1. U.S. Department of Statistics, *www.ahca.org* (Feb. 26, 2002).

2. "How Often the U.S. Population Changes," *USA Today,* June 13, 2002, 1A.

3. For an even more in-depth look at the topic of color analysis, check out *Color Me Beautiful's Looking Your Best: Color, Makeup, and Style* by Mary Spillane and Christine Sherlock (Ballantine Books, 1988).

ABOUT THE AUTHORS

STEVE AND JANIE SJOGREN have been involved in church planting in Oslo, Norway; Baltimore, Maryland; and Cincinnati, Ohio. Janie is a graduate of Sonoma State University (California). Steve graduated from Lutheran Bible Institute of California and Bethany College (Kansas). Together they coauthored *101 Ways to Help People in Need* (NavPress). Steve also has written many books, including *101 Ways to Reach Your Community* (NavPress), *Conspiracy of Kindness,* and *Servant Warfare* (both Vine Books). The Sjogrens live in West Chester, Ohio, with their three children, Rebekah, Laura, and Jack.

ALPHABETICAL LIST OF THE 101 PROJECTS